New Forest
& Isle of Wight

Authors: Helen Livingston and Ann F Stonehouse
Verifier: Ann F Stonehouse
Managing Editor: Paul Mitchell
Art Editor: Carole Philp
Editor: Sandy Draper
Cartography provided by the Mapping Services Department of AA Publishing
Internal colour reproduction: Matt Swann

Produced by AA Publishing
© Automobile Association Developments Limited 2007

 This product includes mapping data licensed from the Ordnance Survey® with the permission of the Controller of Her Majesty's Stationery Office.
© Crown copyright 2007. All rights reserved. Licence number 100021153.

A03033F

TRADE ISBN-13: 978-0-7495-5586-3
SPECIAL ISBN-13: 978-0-7495-5693-8

A CIP catalogue record for this book is available from the British Library.

The contents of this book are believed correct at the time of printing. Nevertheless, the publishers cannot be held responsible for any errors or omissions or for changes in the details given in this book or for the consequences of any reliance on the information it provides. We have tried to ensure accuracy in this book, but things do change and we would be grateful if readers would advise us of any inaccuracies they may encounter. This does not affect your statutory rights.

Visit AA Publishing's website www.theAA.com/travel

Colour reproduction by Keene Group, Andover.
Printed in China by Everbest.

NEW FOREST

CONTENTS

INTRODUCTION

The lure of this beautiful region includes some of the best of rural Hampshire, Wiltshire and Dorset, with many of the south's prettiest villages and most appealing small towns thrown in for good measure. It takes in some of its biggest conurbations, too – sprawling cities such as Southampton, Portsmouth and Bournemouth. It is a region of contrasts and has many aspects: ancient and modern, rural and urban – and in this infinite variety lies its unfailing magic. In the northeast, lies Winchester, Alfred the Great's historic capital, surrounded by water meadows; to the west lies the vast chalk uplands of the Salisbury Plains; in the southwest the Dorset coast and New Forest woodlands and heaths offer plenty to do; while the southeast coast throbs with the great Hampshire ports; and in the distance, lies the many delights of the Isle of Wight.

CRANBORNE

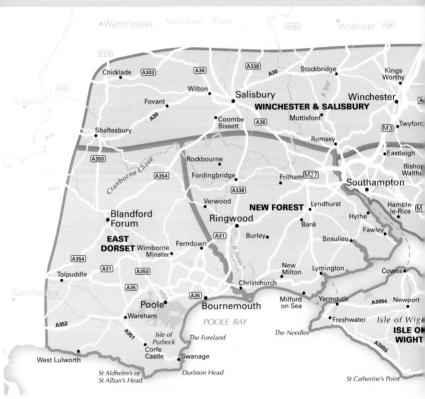

INTRODUCTION

As an area to explore, the lure of the New Forest and the Isle of Wight has plenty to offer discerning visitors. The maritime influence is great here, but there is also forest and heath in which to escape, ancient towns and historic cities to explore, picturesque rural villages to admire, and a coastline and beaches that are unsurpassed. But if, for any reason, you should tire of the mainland, you can always escape to the Isle of Wight. Its miniature coastline has dramatic cliffs and landslips, and impossibly pretty villages.

Back on the mainland, the New Forest, famed for its wildlife conservation and natural beauty, is one of Britain's newest national parks, a status that helps to preserve ancient traditions of land management, and has meant better access than ever for walkers and cyclists. From here, it would be absurd not to venture along the coast to the chalky Jurassic cliffs of east Dorset, celebrated as a World Heritage Site.

Inland there are the winding streams and water meadows of rural Hampshire to discover, and historic Winchester with its squat, medieval cathedral and Jane Austen links. From here, cross into Wiltshire to the busy city of Salisbury, with its soaring Gothic cathedral, or link the two at Romsey, where a massive Norman abbey completes the trio of architectural gems.

If you enjoy stately homes and museums, some of the best in the region are here, including the National Motor Museum at Beaulieu, the Historic Ships collection at Portsmouth, and grand mansions such as Wilton House, Kingston Lacy, Osborne, and the justly famous gardens of Exbury and Mottisfont Abbey. There are glorious, golden sandy beaches at Studland, Swanage and Bournemouth, and inland the superb downs, ancient woodland and open heath to discover.

This guide selects the best of the region and we hope it inspires you to return again and again.

ESSENTIAL SPOTS

If you have little time and you want to sample the essence of the New Forest and its coastline: picnic under a canvas of ancient oaks deep in the forest... join the boating fraternity and sail out of Lymington...visit Osborne House on the Isle of Wight...clamber aboard and imagine life on Nelson's flagship HMS *Victory*...dance the night away in the many bars and clubs of trendy Bournemouth...sunbathe on Studland's beautiful sandy beach...walk among the eerie jagged ruins of Corfe Castle...enjoy a gentle train ride on the busy Alresford–Alton Watercress Line...experience evensong at Winchester Cathedral and marvel at its superb stained-glass windows and interior.

1

2 The Needles
These limestone stacks have long been a welcome sight for weary sailors but many ships have foundered on these dangerous rocks.

3 Calshot
Colourful, traditional seaside huts are a sign of a long-established beach and this is true of Calshot. It is mostly pebbly underfoot.

1 Lulworth Cove/Durdle Door
Crescent-shaped Lulworth Cove is a popular tourist spot now. Its towering limestone cliffs hold the secrets of its history – fossils that tell of a time when dinosaurs wandered the earth, and before, when this part of the south coast was deep under the sea.

4 New Forest Ponies
These friendly little horses have roamed free on their ancient homeland of heath and woods for centuries.

5 Spinnaker Tower
Portsmouth's Spinnaker Tower was the city's main millennium project. It was planned to open in 2000, but the tower didn't open until 2005. The tourist attraction stands 558 feet (170m) high and the viewing platform at the top can be reached by a choice of high-speed or panoramic lifts.

6 Shanklin Chine

A chine is a deep ravine, formed here as water has carved out a narrow path through the stone below. The waterfall is a feature of this lovely area that is known for its variety of wildlife and range of flora.

7 Christchurch Quay

The Avon and the Stour meet at this popular town. The riverfront is dominated by moored craft of varying sizes and condition and there is invariably someone painting or renovating their boats. The river itself is always busy with pleasure craft on tours, and serious sailors heading out to, or returning from, the sea.

Day One in New Forest & Coast

For many people a weekend break or a long weekend is a popular way of spending their leisure time. These pages offer a loosely planned itinerary designed to ensure that you make the most of your time, whatever the weather, and see and enjoy the very best the area has to offer.

Friday Night

Spoil yourself with an overnight stay at the Rhinefield House Hotel, which lies off the A35 southwest of Lyndhurst. It's a Victorian pastiche of a grand Elizabethan mansion, set in several acres of lovely landscaped Italian-style grounds. Relax in the opulent lounge before entering the grand dining hall for dinner – the menu shows French influence, and there's an extensive wine list.

Saturday Morning

After a satisfying breakfast, head into the popular and busy town of Lyndhurst, the so-called 'capital' of the New Forest. Call in at the tourist office beside the main car park and select an area for a morning's walk, or hire a bicycle and follow one of the many waymarked routes. It's by far the best way to see the Forest up close. Don't forget to call in at the Serpentarium, for a sighting of this region's more unusual reptiles.

Saturday Lunch

After your morning's exertions, pick a good country pub for lunch. You're almost spoilt for choice in, but the Royal Oak at Fritham offers a special sort of rural simplicity, and the Trusty Servant at Minstead is always popular, offering a wide range of snacks and full meals.

Saturday Afternoon

After lunch, head west along any of the main routes (the A31–A348–A3049 is probably the least congested), and turn off the A35 at Lytchett Minster for the Isle of Purbeck. Head south, via old Wareham, then pick up the minor road, the B3070, heading down past Lulworth Castle and through Lulworth village to the almost perfect circle of Lulworth Bay. It is worth calling in to the visitor centre here for information about the local geology and fossils, before heading off on a bracing stroll along the cliff path. If it's at all damp underfoot it can be extremely slippery, and walking boots are recommended.

Saturday Evening

As evening settles in, meander through the narrow, winding country lanes to Corfe Castle and beautiful Studland, with its long sandy beach. Cross to Sandbanks on the ferry, and pick out a hotel that most appeals to you – the Harbour Heights, on Haven Road, is a great choice: recently refurbished and chic, it offers fabulous sunset views over Poole harbour from its lovely brasserie terrace, and a stylish, contemporary menu to match.

Day Two in New Forest & Coast

Our second day starts with a visit to the historic port and university town of Portsmouth, with its long-standing importance to the Royal Navy, before driving inland up to the Test Valley and through the market towns of Romsey and Stockbridge on the way to Winchester. End the weekend in this historic city that has fascinating ancient monuments and excellent modern restaurants.

Sunday Morning

After an early breakfast, head northeast from Poole, via Ringwood, on the A31 and then follow the M27 east to junction 7. From here, follow the A334 through the attractive old market towns of Botley and Wickham. Head south on the A32, then follow the A27 eastwards through Portchester and follow the tourist signs south to visit the historic ships collection in Portsmouth. It's unmissable, with a guided tour of Lord Nelson's flagship, HMS *Victory*, the highlight. If you can fit it in, the water-borne tour of the harbour, including views of the ultra-modern Spinnaker Tower, is a must.

Sunday Lunch

You could easily spend the whole day in Portsmouth, but if you want to explore the area further then drive back towards Southampton on the A27. Call in at the village of Hamble or Bursledon for lunch at a traditional waterside pub, and watch the Sunday sailors exercising their craft on the river, with a range of craft from streamlined luxury motor launches to humble dinghies.

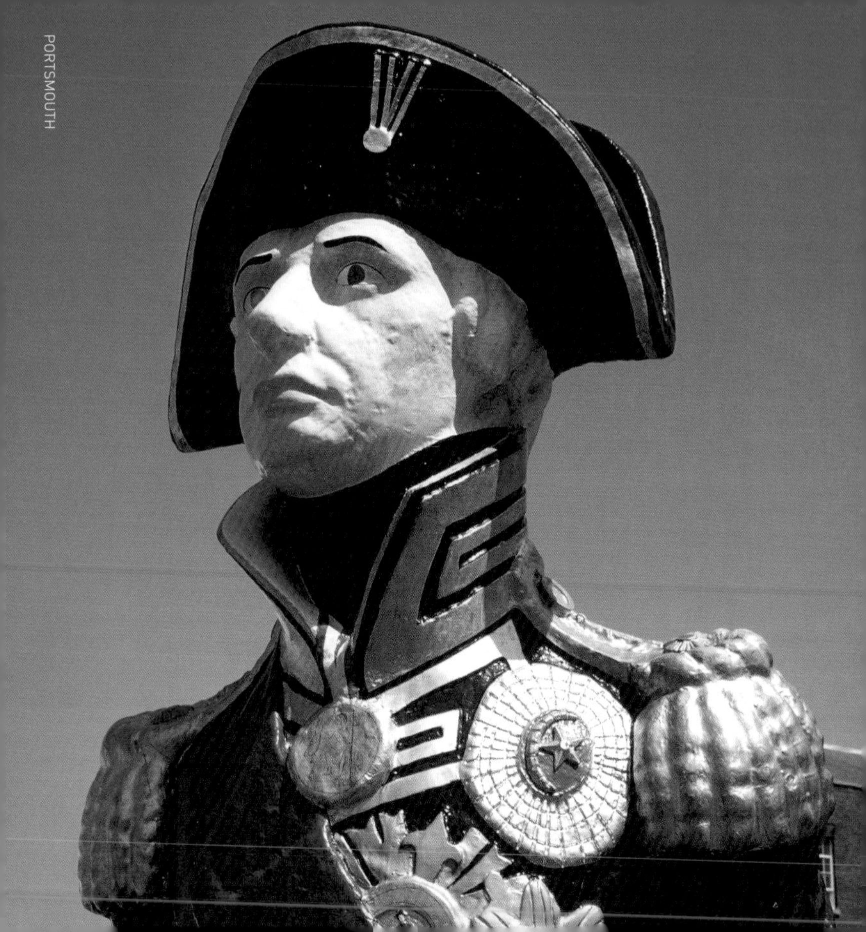

Sunday Afternoon

Return to the M27 and head west, soon turning off at Junction 3 to visit ancient Romsey. Stroll around the town centre and explore the historic abbey, then continue northwards up the A3057 to the venerable town of Stockbridge. A fly-fisherman's delight, Stockbridge has the trout-filled River Test running through it. Enjoy a cup of tea here and perhaps some shopping along the high street, before heading east into Winchester on the B3049.

Sunday Night

There's a great choice places to eat and drink in Winchester, as you'll discover on a pleasant stroll around the city centre when most of the visitors and shoppers have gone for the evening. The elegant Hotel du Vin on Southgate offers cosy, top-notch dining in a friendly but stylish setting, and rooms behind avoid the worst of the town's traffic noise – it's a deservedly popular, if pricey, choice, so book ahead.

341

DOWN BY THE SEA

MUDEFORD

East Dorset

BOURNEMOUTH

BOVINGTON

CORFE CASTLE

CRANBORNE CHASE

KIMMERIDGE BAY

KINGSTON LACY

LULWORTH COVE

MILTON ABBAS

POOLE

STUDLAND

SWANAGE

TOLPUDDLE

WAREHAM

WIMBORNE MINSTER

INTRODUCTION

This region of eastern Dorset incorporates a variety of impossibly pretty, pocket-size villages and towns, and a stretch of coastline that is famous for its fossil cliffs and is dubbed England's Jurassic Coast. With chalky downland, the woodland of Cranbourne Chase, the high ridges of the Purbeck Hills and the glorious golden sands of Studland and Bournemouth, there is plenty of variation in the landscape too. Follow in the footsteps of Lawrence of Arabia, the Tolpuddle Martyrs and the thjnovelist and poet, Thomas Hardy, who immortalised a still recognisable Dorset.

Unmissable attractions

Walk along the golden, sandy beaches of Bournemouth or Studland...climb up to explore the haunting ruins of Corfe Castle...visit the grand 17th-century mansion of Kingston Lacy...marvel at the rock formations in Lulworth Cove and the stone arch of Durdle Door that sits just off its beach...take part in a nostalgic Punch and Judy show while enjoying an ice cream on the Victorian pier in Swanage...act out the part of an army commander and climb aboard an authentic tank at Bovington's fascinating Tank Museum...picnic in the rolling grasslands of Cranborne Chase surrounded by a mist of colourful butterflies...fill up on fish and chips at Poole's thriving quayside.

1

1 Corfe Castle
The castle was destroyed during the Civil War after a long siege. Then, the defenders were allowed to leave once the castle was damaged beyond repair, in order to prevent its further use.

2 Bournemouth Pier
The pier underwent a costly renovation in the early 1980s and is now an essential attraction along Bournemouth's seafront.

3 Lulworth Cove
Although popular with those who favour paddling and sitting by the sea, the area surrounding Lulworth Cove and Durdle Door is wonderful for anyone who prefers to walk and enjoy the variety of landscape here including open spaces and narrow, chalk paths.

4

4 Kingston Lacy

The wealthy Bankes family built Kingston Lacy as their new home after their family seat, Corfe Castle, was destroyed in the Civil War. This grand mansion has been renovated and houses a renowned collection of paintings.

5 Cranborne Chase

The Chase is part of the UK's sixth largest Area of Oustanding Natural Beauty and is characterised by gently rolling chalk slopes.

5

6 Poole

Poole's large natural harbour determined its future as a port, and made it an important centre for boat and yacht building. Poole quay is usually busy with visitors and locals, whereas the old part of the harbour is much quieter.

BOURNEMOUTH

Bournemouth is the queen of the south coast holiday resorts, with its 6 miles (9.6km) of fine golden sands, its pier complete with striped deck chairs and theatre for nostalgic summer shows, its orderly winter gardens, its palm-tree lined parks and compact town centre dedicated to serious shopping.

Unlike its more serious neighbour, Poole, Bournemouth has never really been anything other than a resort. It was a small village in the early 19th century, at the time when many of the pine trees that now scent the air were first planted. Blessed with a mild climate, and a south-facing location in a sheltered cleft, the settlement boomed towards the end of the 19th century, and most of the town's central buildings date from this period, with Victorian buildings interspersed with some later Art Deco. New luxury blocks of offices and modern accommodation may have changed the skyline for ever, but the towns heart has a comfortable, old-fashioned feel that still appeals to many holiday-makers The town centre is shaped around the Lower, Centre and Upper Gardens, a long, leafy park around the flowing Bourne stream, with magnificent island flowerbeds, scenic tethered balloon flights, an aviary, a mini-golf centre and various refreshment stops. Around the upper end and the Square cluster all the main shopping streets, with arcades

BEACH HUTS

These wooden chalets are an integral feature of seaside resorts, and date back to the days when sea-bathers were taken modestly out into the shallows in horse-drawn wooden huts on wheels, before entering the water in full costume. Today they offer a bit of home on the beach, and sell for tens of thousands of pounds. At Bournemouth, however, you can rent them by the day – ask at the tourist office.

BOURNEMOUTH

leading off the largely pedestrianised Old Christchurch Road. The most appealing of these is the glazed 1866 Victorian Arcade housing the well-known Dingles department store and designer outlets including Gucci and Karen Millen. Beales is Bournemouth's largest independent department store. Opposite it is St Peter's Church, with Arts and Crafts wall paintings, a chapel dedicated to the Oxford Movement reformer John Keble, and the grave of Gothic novelist Mary Shelley (and heart of her brother the Romantic poet) in the churchyard.

The lower end of the park runs past the Pavilion Theatre, under the main road and out onto the seafront, with the pier just ahead. Bournemouth's pier is a functional affair, reinforced with ugly concrete that has seen it survive when others along this coastline have been washed away. Photographs at the far end show how it was partly demolished during World War II to prevent its use in a possible German invasion. Now it has a pier theatre and amusements, and great views back to the town, and the western beaches with their beach huts tucked under the sandy cliffs. A land train offers transport up and down the seafront. The twin domes near the pier entrance mark the aquarium, and the modern glazed building on the seafront is the IMAX cinema complex. Set behind this, on the East Cliff, you will find the turreted Russell-Cotes Art Gallery and Museum, which is home to a collection of Victorian paintings and treasures from around the world.

BOVINGTON

The Royal Artillery, the Infantry and the Royal Armoured Corps train their drivers on a six-million pound, all-weather circuit near Bovington, and there has been military training in the area since the first tanks were introduced during World War I. Bovington's Tank Museum explains it all, and has the world's largest collection of around 250 armoured fighting vehicles, and exhibits from 25 countries – you don't even have to be a tank fanatic to enjoy it. Mock battles and rides are offered in summer. One corner is devoted to 'Lawrence of Arabia', who has strong links to this part of Dorset. In nearby Moreton churchyard is a slab of white marble inscribed: 'To the dear memory of T E Lawrence, Fellow of All Souls College, Oxford. Born 16 August 1888, died 19 May 1935.'

The brilliant, enigmatic and haunted figure of Lawrence continues to intrigue people. As British liaison officer to the Arab Revolt, Lawrence proved himself a leader with an ambitious personality and an extensive knowledge of strategic warfare. His flamboyant courage and adoption of Arabic dress gave him heroic status when Akaba was captured in 1917, and Damascus achieved in the following year. Lawrence remained involved in Arab affairs even after the war, lobbying unsuccessfully for Arab independence. Finding fame a

Visit

MORETON GLASS

Moreton church was rebuilt after bomb damage in 1940, and its chief delight is its windows. What from outside looks like plain glass, from inside it is revealed to be engraved with a vivid flow of delicate pictorial designs. The etching is the work of the late Lawrence Whistler (more of his work can be seen in Salisbury Cathedral). The window (1982) in the Trinity Chapel particularly rewards closer inspection; it is an anonymous memorial to an airman killed over France during the war, and tells of a brief marriage cut short, illustrated by magnolia blossoms, a sunburst, and a crashed biplane.

millstone, he joined the ranks of the RAF in 1922, seeking a degree of security and regular life as Aircraftsman Ross.

Discovered, he first enlisted in the Tank Corps at Bovington in 1923 as Private T E Shaw, and moved to Dorset, buying a derelict house at nearby Clouds Hill (now National Trust) as an evening and weekend retreat. Clouds Hill is a bachelor house, with a gramophone, well-stocked book shelves, comfortable firesides and few frills; it became his 'earthly paradise'. Lawrence finished writing his account of the Arab Revolt, *The Seven Pillars of Wisdom* (1926) and in 1925 rejoined the RAF.

In 1935 he retired to Clouds Hill, but on 13 May that year, returning home on his Brough Superior SS-100, he swerved to avoid cyclists and was thrown from the motorcycle. He died five days later; the legend is still very much alive.

CORFE CASTLE

Corfe is the best-known village on the so-called Isle of Purbeck, and is packed with pubs, tea rooms and little shops making it a magnet for summer visitors, who are rewarded with excellent walking in the area.

The huge ruin of Corfe Castle seems to perfectly fill the gap in the wall of the Purbeck Hills with its presence. It has a grim history. In AD 978 a youthful King Edward (the Martyr) was cruelly murdered here by his stepmother; his body was buried without ceremony at Wareham, while his half-brother took the throne as Ethelred II (the Unready). However, stories of miracles soon resulted in the exhumation of Edward's body. It was transported to Shaftesbury, where an abbey grew up in his honour.

Around 1106 the big square Norman keep was built, to defend against raiders from the sea and to impress the local populace. King John used it as a lifelong prison for his niece Eleanor, a potential threat to his throne. Edward II, deposed by his wife, was imprisoned here briefly.

During the Civil War the castle's owner, Sir John Bankes, eventually sided with the King, leaving his spirited wife Mary, with a handful of women and just five men, to fight off a siege in 1642. History books state that the 500-strong Parliamentarian army stripped all the lead from the

THE GREYHOUND

church roof to make their bullets, and stored their gunpowder and shot in the organ pipes, but they failed to take the castle. After a second siege, the castle was betrayed in 1646 by one of its defenders, and after it was abandoned it was destroyed to prevent its use again.

South of Corfe, Worth Matravers is a picturesque village of lichen-encrusted grey cottages, complete with a duck pond. Men from here have worked in the local quarries for centuries, and Purbeck marble (in fact a type of limestone) from this area was famously sent inland for the building of the magnificent Salisbury Cathedral. The Square & Compass, an old-fashioned pub with smoked beams and a big stone hearth, is a favourite with walkers. On the nearby cliffs stands 800-year-old St Adhelm's Chapel, a sturdy, buttressed brown cube, that has only one tiny little window. Near the coastguard station is a steel memorial to the brilliant work of radar developers here in 1940–42.

CRANBORNE CHASE

Cranborne Chase covers an area of around 100sq miles (260sq km) of the long chalk massif which straddles the Dorset–Wiltshire border to the east of Shaftesbury. It was once a popular royal hunting preserve, but is now mostly rolling grassland with pockets of mixed woodland. On the northwestern flanks, Fontmell and Melbury Downs are particularly beautiful, and covered with butterflies in summer. To the southeast lie a string of attractive little villages, including Tarrants Gunville and Hinton, and Chettle. Sixpenny Handley has one of the oddest names in England – which alone justifies a visit – but if you go there expecting a romantic 1950s throwback, be prepared for a surprise. Much of the old village was destroyed by fire in 1892; today it is a bold, lively modern village with lots of new housing.

Compared with other parts of Dorset, there are few settlements here, a sign of the feudal state in which the land was held until 1830. After the last Ice Age, Dorset was smothered in a growth of broadleaved woodland, including species such as oak, ash and elm, known as 'native'. As the human population grew and spread, this woodland was gradually cleared for its timber and to make way for agricultural land. The hunting 'forest' of Cranborne Chase claimed by William the Conqueror therefore included wide, open sections of heath, downland, scrub and rough pasture, as well as patches of remaining woodland.

Little of the original forest remains on the Chase – most woods show signs of mixed planting and many generations of coppicing, which was designed to produce a continuous supply of timber for everyday use. The effects of planting for timber in the later 18th century can be seen in the widespread stands of non-native beech across the Chase. Trees for timber were planted compactly to encourage tall, straight growth with a minimum of interruption from side branches. The pursuit of fallow deer on the Chase provided the mainstay of royal sport, and they can still be seen here, most visible in the early evening.

In the early 18th century, the hunting rights on Cranborne Chase passed to the powerful Pitt-Rivers family, who proceeded to rule the area like a feudal manor. Operating under the so-called Chase Law it became a byway for many smugglers

Visit

SMEDMORE HOUSE

The Clavell family have been at Smedmore since the 13th century, and Smedmore House, a handsome twin-bayed affair dating from 1761, keeps a firm eye on activities in the bay still. It is occasionally open in high summer when its attractive gardens are in bloom. The Clavell Tower folly, now dangerously close to the crumbling cliff edge, is currently the subject of a major rescue project.

41

and a refuge for criminals. In 1830, after much local campaigning, Chase Law was abandoned.

KIMMERIDGE BAY

There's a lovely bleakness about Kimmeridge Bay which the energy of the youthful windsurfers riding the waves and the cheerful picture of families pottering in the rock pools can't quite dispel. Giant slabs of black rock shelving out to sea, with crumbling cliffs topped by clumps of wild cabbage, create something of this mood, and the slow, steady nodding donkey-head of the oil well above a terrace of unmistakably industrial cottages reinforces it.

Iron Age tribes first spotted the potential of the band of bituminous shale that runs through Kimmeridge, polishing it up into different blackstone ornaments, and even chair and table legs. The shale, permeated with crude oil, is also known as Kimmeridge coal, but many attempts to work it on an industrial scale failed, including alum extraction (for dyeing) in the 16th century, and using the coal to fuel a glassworks in the 17th century. The shale was worked in the 19th century, and for one brief period the street lights of Paris were lit by gas extracted from the shale oil, but nothing lasted for very long. Since 1959 British Petroleum has drilled 1,716 feet (520m) below the sea; its beam engine sucks out some 80 barrels of crude oil a day. Transported to the Wytch Farm collection point, near Corfe, the oil is then pumped to Hamble, ready to be shipped around the world.

Its combination of clear, shallow water, double low tides and accessible rocky ledges make Kimmeridge an ideal choice for an underwater nature reserve. The double low tide is at its best in the afternoons – effectively, the water may stay low all afternoon, allowing optimum access to the fingers of rock that stretch out into the bay, revealing an amazing world of rock pools and gullies alive with

seaweeds, anemones and creatures that include crabs, blennies and the more bizarre pipe-fish. Learn more at the Fine Foundation Marine Centre. Kimmeridge is part of the Smedmore estate, and accessed via a private toll road.

In contrast to Kimmeridge, just over the hill lies Tyneham, a cosy farming village clustered around its church in a glorious valley. As you get up close, however, you realise that it's uncannily neat, like a film set from the 40s – Greer Garson's Mrs Miniver could appear at any moment. There's a spreading oak tree by the church gate, a quaint old phone box; even a village pump. The stone cottages are newly repointed, but roofless. And the church, as you enter on a chilly mid-winter day is warm! Inside the church is an exhibition to explain all: the villagers were asked to give up their homes in December 1943 for the 'war effort', and Tyneham became absorbed into the vast acreage of the Lulworth Ranges, part of the live firing range.

It is a touching memorial, though perhaps nothing can make up for the fact that the villagers were never allowed back to their homes. Emerging again, you half expect to see soldiers popping out of the windows, but relax, you can only visit when the ranges are closed.

KINGSTON LACY

Kingston Lacy is an impossibly elegant mansion dating from 1663 and is set in extensive parkland northwest of Wimborne. The house, which has a particularly fine collection of paintings, was built for the Bankes family after the destruction of Corfe Castle in the Civil War, and the house was then remodelled in the 19th century by Sir Charles Barry. One of the most unusual chambers is the Spanish Room, with its walls adorned with gilded leather. On the 8,000-acre (3,240ha) estate, Conegar Capers is a woodland play area for younger children, and there are lots of good waymarked walks.

One of the most obvious legacies of the Roman invasion of Britain in AD 43 is the network of straight military roads that they constructed across the country. Four of the most important Roman routes met at the hub of Badbury Rings, just north of Kingston Lacy. The most famous and visible of these is Ackling Dyke, the major road which linked London (*Londinium*) with Old Sarum (*Sorviodunum*), Dorchester (*Durnovaria*, the civitas or Roman capital of the Dorset area) and Exeter (Iscarduniorum).

Badbury Rings was a massive hill-fort occupying a spectacular vantage point. Bronze Age burial barrows in the area confirm a settlement in around 2000 BC, and the rings and ditches date from the 6th century BC, when Dorset was inhabited by the Durotriges tribe. It is a peaceful spot, softened by the trees, a recent replanting to replicate what was there in 1761. The hill-fort is approached via an avenue of beeches planted by William Bankes.

LULWORTH COVE

Lulworth Cove is an almost perfectly circular bay in the rolling line of limestone cliffs that form Dorset's southern coast. It provides a safe anchorage for small fishing boats and pleasure craft, and a sun-trap of safe water for summer bathers. The wave-polished grey, black and red pebbles of the shingle beach, from wren's egg to ostrich egg in size, are reminiscent of childhood jars of pebble sweets. To the west, along the South West Coast Path, lie rolling, chalky downs and the landmark of Durdle Door, below the cliffs. To the east lie the delightful Worbarrow and Mupe bays. The geology of the area is intriguing, and a visit to the Heritage Centre in the village will help you to identify the various rock formations. The oldest layer is the gleaming white Portland stone, much employed by Christopher Wren in his rebuilding of London. It is a fine-grained oolite around 140 million years old, consisting of tightly

compressed fossilised shells, and occasionally throws up giant flat-coiled ammonites, called a titanite, which may be seen incorporated decoratively into many house walls across Purbeck. Above this is a thick layer of Purbeck marble, a rich limestone where dinosaur, reptile and fish fossils are usually found. The soft layer above this consists of Wealden beds – a belt of colourful sedimentary clays, silts and sands that are unstable and prone to landslips when exposed. Crumbly white chalk overlays this, the remains of microscopic sea creatures and shells deposited over a long period of time when a deep sea covered much of Dorset, some 75 million years ago.

The Fossil Forest in the sea cliffs east of Lulworth Cove is an intriguing oddity, but don't go looking for stone trees. What you see are the stone rings where sediment has bubbled up around tree trunks that rotted away millions of years ago. Together with the fossilised soil

discovered beneath the tree boles, they give an insight into Jurassic life here, 135 million years ago.

Lulworth Castle Park at East Lulworth was a hunting lodge, built four-square in 1608 with pepperpot towers. Gutted by fire in 1929, it is now a, partly restored if handsome, shell. Other attractions on the estate include a chapel, an animal farm, an adventure playground and summer jousting events.

THE DOLLS HOUSE

As you make your way down to the pretty harbour in Lulworth, look out for the tiny baby-blue painted timber Dolls House. It is a restored Victorian fisherman's cottage dating from 1861, now a fishing museum, and you may find it difficult to believe that 11 children were raised in this tiny house. Contrast its cramped simplicity with the cottage orné opposite, complete with big diamond-pane windows and a cosy thatched roof.

Nearly 200 rescued and endangered apes and monkeys have found a new, welcoming home at Monkey World, a few miles north of Wool. The park has of 65 acres (26ha) of woodland, where the monkeys can recuperate in a safe, purpose-built environment.

MILTON ABBAS

It is the natural order of villages to grow over generations, to spread out a little, to develop secret corners, and to reflect different ages, abilities and tastes in its buildings. Rarely do you find a village quite so symmetrical as Milton Abbas, whose whitewashed houses, identical in design, are placed neatly on either side of a narrow defile, thatched cowl opposite thatched cowl. It's an unnatural and slightly eerie sight. On closer inspection, you see that rebels have managed to sneak on a porch here, a coat of cream-coloured paint there, but nothing to seriously spoil the effect of planned perfection. There appear to have been no concessions either on houses that were once a bakery and a forge, although the tailor's house had bow windows for extra light.

The answer lies with the great house round the corner, the dream of Joseph and Caroline Damer, who bought Milton Abbey in 1752. It was on a fabulous site, but the house left much to be desired. In 1771 they decided to build something grander, to include a landscaped park by 'Capability' Brown. But the ugly and untidy township around the abbey was spoiling the view, and would have to go.

And so a new hamlet of thatched cottages was built out of sight in a narrow valley, and the villagers were moved, whether they liked it or not. The houses look generous, but in fact each little block was two independent family dwellings, separated by a shared central hall. What the villagers had to say about the near-vertical valley walls behind their shiny new homes is not recorded, but some steep terraced gardens were eventually dug out, and are one of the attractive features of Milton Abbas today.

The Damers are buried in splendour in the abbey church; their house, never the architectural success they had hoped for, became a school in 1954.

Nearby Winterborne Clenston is altogether more organic, combining a pretty Victorian rectory with a fine Tudor manor house and a medieval tithe barn with a steep chequer-board roof of alternating red and black squares. The Gothic church of St Nicholas, dating from 1840, is a perfectly proportioned miniature.

POOLE

Unlike its more frivolous and glitzy neighbour Bournemouth, Poole has an ancient and serious heart that gives it a different character.

It grew up in the Middle Ages as the main port on one of the world's greatest and safest natural harbours, taking over in maritime importance from Wareham. Today it is still very much a working port, with marinas packed out with expensive sailing yachts, a small surviving fishing fleet, many productive boatyards creating some of the most expensive and sleekest luxury motorboats made in the world, and cross-Channel ferries – the biggest craft to negotiate the narrow entrance to the impressive harbour at Sandbanks.

The best place to start exploring Old Poole is the Quayside – the attractive old waterfront, with views across the harbour and more immediately, to the boatyards. The Cockle Trail is a walk around the historic town – pick up a leaflet at the tourist office.

At the western end, the Quay is lined with stylish old buildings, including the brick Customs House of 1813, as well as the pillared Coastguard office of 1820, all on an appealingly small scale. There are old pubs along here too, including the Poole Arms with is green-glazed tile frontage, and the handsome

King's Head, set slightly back at the lower end of the High Street. This is Poole's main shopping street, lined with small and largely practical shops – for bigger high-street names head inland to the modern Dolphin Shopping Centre. As you stroll eastwards along the Quay, past the town marina with its gleaming moored yachts, you soon reach the rustier hulks of the fishing fleet. There is a small museum in a wooden shed to explore, its paint faded and peeling – it is the home of the old Thomas Kirk Wright lifeboat, which took part as one of the flotilla of 'Little Ships' in the brave evacuation of Allied soldiers from Dunkirk in May, 1940.

Between the Quay and the end tip of the sheltering sandspit of Sandbanks, the coastline seems like one long haven or park dedicated to varied watersports and sailing. Paragliding, wakeboarding and kitesurfing are favourite activities in these shallow, sheltered waters. Laid inland from Sandbanks amid elegant and spacious Edwardian villas, Compton Acres is a huge, privately owned pleasure garden established in the 1920s. As well as themed gardens which include a Wooded Valley, a pretty Grotto, a Water Garden, Roman and Japanese gardens, the 10-acre (4ha) site also has two restaurants, a delicatessen, craft and gift shops.

Poole Pottery is 4 miles (6.5km) from the Old Town, and offers factory tours, or pop into the factory outlet on the Quay, where you can paint your own plate or bowl.

STUDLAND

The glorious sands in Studland Bay are justly famous, and attract over a million visitors a year, so it's worth getting up early to have them to yourself. You are unlikely to be alone for long, though.

As you progress up the beach, getting warmer, you can shed your clothes with impunity, for the upper stretch opens its arms to naturists – and even on a bright

STUDLAND

Insight

EDGAR 'TAFFY' EVANS

On Swange High Street, the small terraced house at No 82A bears a modest metal plaque above the front door, announcing that this was the home of Petty Officer Edgar 'Taffy' Evans. An experienced seaman, he was described by a companion as a 'giant worker'. He perished with Captain Scott from the effects of frostbite and exhaustion on his way back from the South Pole in 1912.

winter's morning you'll spot a few brave souls sunbathing naked in the shelter of the marram-covered dunes. Off shore, big, sleek motor boats let rip as they emerge from the constraints of Poole Harbour. Watch out, too, for the orange and blue of the Poole lifeboat on manoeuvres, and the yellow and black pilot boat nipping out to lead in the tankers. Jet-skiers zip around the more sedate sailing yachts, all dodging the small fishing boats. It's a perfect seaside harmony, complete with wheeling, soaring gulls.

Studland's sand is pale gold and fine-ground, trodden by thousands of feet, piled into sand castles and smoothed daily by the sea. It's a wonderful place for shell spotting. Look for the flattish, conical mother-of-pearl whorls of tops shells, the curious pinky-brown pockets of slipper limpets, the glossy, uneven orange disks of the common saddle oyster and the flat reddish-brown sun-rays of scallops. The deeply ridged fans of common cockles and the vivid blue flash of mussels are a common sight. More challenging is to identify the uneven ellipse of sand gapers or the delicate finger-nail pink of the thin tellin.

Behind the beach lies the old rugged heath, part of the same nature reserve that is in the care of English Nature and the National Trust. They are currently working together on a programme of restoration, reclaiming heath that had become farmland, and clearing scrub and maintaining controlled grazing to prevent it all reverting to woodland. All six of Britain's reptiles – common lizard, sand lizard, smooth snake, adder, grass snake, slow worm – live on the heath.

SWANAGE

In the early 19th century Swanage was a small, bustling industrial port shipping stone from the 60 or more quarries in the area. A growing fashion for sea-bathing would in time change the focus of the town for ever. The real changes to the face of Swanage came, however, with the extraordinary collecting habit of one George Burt, a contractor with an eye for ornate architecture.

With his uncle John Mowlem, a local stonemason and philanthropist, Burt shipped marble from the old quarries of Purbeck up to London, where many old buildings were being knocked down to make way for new construction. He was reluctant to see such fine stonework discarded, so Burt salvaged large whole pieces,

transported them back to Dorset as ballast, and re-erected them in his home town, giving Swanage an 'instant' architectural heritage.

The Town Hall is a prime example of Burt's influence. He had donated a reasonably plain and simple building to the town in 1872; but in 1883 he added a façade by Wren, which he had rescued from the Mercers' Hall in London's Cheapside. In a park near the pier you can see a grand archway removed from Hyde Park Corner, and three statues and some columns rescued from Billingsgate Market. There is also an absurd but rather elegant clock tower, removed from the south end of London Bridge in 1867, where it had been set as a memorial to the Duke of Wellington.

Durleston Castle is an original folly by Burt dating from 1887, designed from the start as a cliff-top restaurant on Durleston Head. Facts and figures from around the world are carved into great stone slabs set into the walls below. Burt added

PUNCH & JUDY
SWANAGE
SHOWS DAILY
12.30 2.30 4.00

Adults & Children
£1.00

a large, segmented stone globe of the world. It is grey and rather disappointing, but nevertheless in a beautiful spot where you can sit watching the sunset fade the sea into the sky, with the lighthouse at the end of the Needles winking from across the water.

At Studland Museum and Heritage Centre you can learn more about the area, including tales of smuggling and the development of Purbeck's stone quarrying industry. And for a nominal fee, try the delights of Swanage's Victorian pier, which announces penny-in-the-slot machines and 'Wot the butler saw' – no seaside visit can be complete without it. The pier suffered in the past from neglect and threat of demolition, but is now undergoing extensive restoration.

TOLPUDDLE

Tolpuddle is a peaceful village tucked in the fold of a hill beside the A35. It is associated with a political revolt in the 19th century, celebrated with the Martyrs' Museum, commemorated in the name of the local pub, and at various other points.

The Martyrs' Tree stands on the little green at the heart of Tolpuddle. It was a meeting point for the Friendly Society of Agricultural Labourers, a group formed to peaceably lobby their masters for much better pay, at a time when a local labourer's wage was just seven shillings a week – around three shillings below what was paid elsewhere in Dorset, and barely enough to feed a family on. Such unions were unlawful, and George and James Loveless, Thomas and John Standfield, James Brine and James Hammett were picked out as ringleaders and troublemakers, and convicted at Dorchester in 1834.

The six men were duly exiled, but their case was unusual. Despite their conviction for 'administering unlawful oaths', their seven-year sentences were quashed after public outrage, and the Tolpuddle Martyrs were pardoned. The processes of law and communication were slow in those times, and it was five years before they all returned home.

George Loveless, a well-spoken Methodist lay preacher whose statue sits outside the museum, had developed a taste for life beyond these valleys, and after his return he emigrated to Canada with four of the others. James Hammet was the only one to die in the village, and his grave is in the local churchyard. The story of the Tolpuddle Martyrs serves as a chilling reminder of the 1,800 individuals convicted of political crimes between 1800 and 1850, who were shipped out to Australia, effectively silencing so-called dangerous elements.

Athelhampton, one of England's most majestic old mansions, lies just to the west of Tolpuddle. Parts of it date from 1485, and the house is stuffed with treasures, from Tudor architecture in the Great Hall to a carved Charles I tester bed. Allow plenty of time to explore the world-famous gardens with superb yew topiary and fountains.

Insight

T E LAWRENCE

The sculptured effigy of Lawrence was made between 1936 and 1939 by Eric Kennington, the official war artist, and was intended to be a memorial to stand in St Paul's Cathedral, London. However, on Lawrence's death St Paul's, then Westminster Abbey and finally Salisbury Cathedral all turned it down, and the ancient church at Wareham became its less glamourous home.

WAREHAM

Wareham bills itself as a Saxon walled town, but a devastating fire in 1762 destroyed many of the older buildings, and what you see today in the town centre is mainly Georgian. Wareham has had a chequered history, its status as the major trading port on Poole Harbour making it quite vulnerable to attacks from marauding Vikings, and then undermined when the River Frome silted up during the Middle Ages.

One survivor from the town's earliest heyday is St Martin's Church. Dating from around 1030, it's the oldest church in Dorset, and stands on the northern section of the ancient town walls. It has some remarkable fragments of 12th-century frescoes, and now houses an effigy of T E Lawrence, by sculptor Eric Kennington, in Arab costume and with his head resting on a camel saddle. Learn more about Lawrence of Arabia in the redbrick Town Museum on the High Street. This broad and gracious street is the main thoroughfare of the town, leading down to the river, and is lined with plenty of interesting shops and eating places.

Stroll along the quiet heath road through Ridge, once a busy river port in its own right, to the hamlet of Arne, 3 miles (4.8km) away near the shores of Poole Harbour. Many of the houses here were demolished during World War II when the army used the village as a training ground, and what's left remains in sleepy retirement. There is a 13th-century church to explore, and a nature reserve where rare Dartford warblers breed and nightjars sing.

North of Wareham, at Sandford, is Farmer Palmer's, a great family farm park with hands-on animal feeding, milking cows, tractor rides and amusements.

WIMBORNE MINSTER

This attractive old market town made its fortunes in ancient times on the profits of wool. Its most distinctive feature is the Minster Church of St Cuthberga, whose squat, square towers dominate the town centre. Its foundation dates back to AD 705, though the present building dates from some 400 years later. One of the town's most fascinating elements is the library, founded in 1686 for the free use of the townspeople, and consisting of 350 (mainly theological) volumes. To prevent theft, the books were chained to the shelves – workhouse orphans made the chains. The

WAREHAM

Insight

THE RIVER STOUR

The Stour supports a rich variety of wildlife. Most obvious are the birds, with mallards and mute swans on the water, moorhens, warblers and buntings in the tall reed beds, and grey herons and exotic white egrets fishing in the shallows. Trout, roach, perch, dace, minnows and eels live in the water, and in summer look out for orange tip, peacock and clouded yellow butterflies, dragonflies and damselflies.

Quarter Jack clock on the west tower is a much-loved local icon, with its brightly painted soldier striking the quarter hours.

The nearby village Cornmarket, is a sheltered square, with an old pub, the White Hart, that becomes the centre of activities around the Folk Festival. The King's Head Hotel on the old main Square was formerly a coaching inn. The Priest's House Museum on the High Street is a medieval house, originally built for use by the priests at the Minster but was later occupied by a succession of different tradespeople, including an ironmonger, a tobacconist and a printer. It is full of the domestic paraphernalia of years gone by, including a Victorian kitchen and a tinsmith's workshop. The walled garden, which leads gently down to the river, is a particular delight.

Wimborne has its own model town, carefully created to 1/10 scale some 50 years ago and set in lovely gardens. As well as a model railway, putting lawn and special events.

East of Wimborne, at Hampreston, lie Knoll Gardens, a superb modern garden and specialist nursery displaying grasses, perennials and much more. To the northeast lies Stapehill, the site of a 19th-century abbey now transformed into extensive, beautiful formal as well as informal gardens, with a countryside museum and farmyard. There are also resident craftspeople, industrial cottages reinforces it.

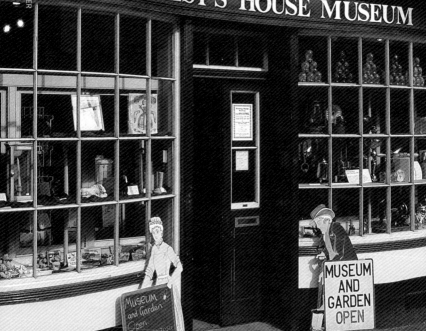

THE PRIEST'S HOUSE MUSEUM

Museum
and Garden
Open.

MUSEUM
AND
GARDEN
OPEN

TOURIST INFORMATION CENTRES

Bournemouth
Westover Road.
Tel: 0845 051 1700;
www.bournemouth.co.uk

Poole
Enefco House, Poole Quay.
Tel: 01202 253253;
www.pooletourism.com

Swanage
The White House,
Shore Road.
Tel: 01929 422885;
www.swanage.gov.uk

Wareham
Holy Trinity Church,
South Street.
Tel: 01929 522740;
www.purbeck.gov.uk

Wimborne
29 High Street.
Tel: 01202 886116;
www.ruraldorset.com

PLACES OF INTEREST

Arne RSPB Reserve
Wareham.
Tel: 01929 553360

Athelhampton House & Gardens
Tel: 01305 848363;
www.athelhampton.co.uk

Bournemouth Aviation Museum
Bournemouth Airport.
Tel: 01202 580858;
www.aviation-museum.co.uk

Bovington Tank Museum
Tel: 01929 405096;
www.tankmuseum.org

Brownsea Island (NT)
Offshore Poole Harbour.
Tel: 01202 707744

Clouds Hill (NT)
Near Bovington. Tel: 01929 405616

Compton Acres
Tel: 01202 700778;
www.comptonacres.co.uk

Corfe Castle (NT)
Tel: 01929 481294

Corfe Model Village
Tel: 01929 481234;
www.corfecastlemodelvillage.co.uk

Fine Foundation Marine Centre
Purbeck Marine Wildlife Reserve,
Kimmeridge Bay.
Tel: 01929 481044

Kingston Lacy (NT)
Wimborne Minster. Tel: 01202 883402
Knoll Gardens
Hampreston, nr Wimborne.
Tel: 01202 873931;
www.knollgardens.co.uk
Lulworth Castle & Park
East Lulworth, Wareham.
Tel: 0845 450 1054; www.lulworth.com
Monkey World
Wool, near Wareham.
Tel: 0800 456600;
www.monkeyworld.org
Oceanarium
Pier Approach, West Beach,
Bournemouth.
Tel: 01202 311993;
www.oceanarium.co.uk
Old Poole Lifboat Museum
The Quay, Poole.
Poole Pottery
Sopers Lane, Poole. Tel: 01202 666200;
www.poolepottery.com
Priest's House Museum
& Garden
23–27 High Street, Wimborne Minster.
Tel: 01202 882533;
www.priest-house.co.uk

Swanage Museum
& Heritage Centre
Tel: 01929 421427;
www.swanagemuseum.org.uk
Swanage Railway
Tel: 01929 425800;
www.swanagerailway.co.uk
Tolpuddle Martyrs' Museum
Tel: 01305 848237
Wareham Town Museum
Town Hall, East Street.
Tel: 01929 533448
Waterfront Museum
Poole.
Tel: 01202 262600

FOR CHILDREN
Adventure Wonderland
Hurn. Tel: 01202 483444;
www.adventurewonderland.co.uk
Farmer Palmer's
Wareham Road, Organford, Poole.
Tel: 01202 622022;
www.farmerpalmers.co.uk
Model Town
Wimborne Minster.
Tel: 01202 881924;
www.wimborne-modeltown.com

63

EAST DORSET

Splashdown Water Park
Tower Park, northeast of Poole on
A3049. Tel: 01202 716000;
www.splashdownpoole.com

SHOPPING
Poole Markets
Street market, High Street, and
Farmer's Market, Falkland Square,
every Thu.
Swanage Market & Farmers' Market
Main beach car park, Tue, Easter–
Autumn.
Wareham Market
Every Thu.
Wimborne Market & Farmers' Market
Friday; also flea market Sat–Sun.

PERFORMING ARTS
Pavilion Theatre
Westover Road, Bournemouth.
Tel: 01202 456400
Bournemouth International Centre
Exeter Road.
Tel: 01202 456400
Pier Theatre
Exeter Road, Bournemouth.
Tel: 01202 456 456

SPORTS & ACTIVITIES
Adrenalin Days
A variety of powerboat and charter boat
trips that leave from Poole Harbour.
Tel: 07881 586575
Christchurch Ski & Leisure Centre
Matchams Lane, Hurn.
Tel: 01202 499155;
www.christchurch-skicentre.com
Shockwave
Speedboat tours of the bay.
Bournemouth Pier.
Tel: 01202 558550;
www.dorsetcruises.co.uk

CRUISES & FERRIES
Blue Line Cruises
Sailings from Poole Quay.
Tel: 0800 096 0695/01202 467882;
www.bluelinecruises.co.uk
Brownsea Island Ferries Ltd
Tel: 01929 462383;
www.brownseaislandferries.com
The Dorset Belles
Bournemouth Pier.
Tel: 01202 558550;
www.dorsetcruises.co.uk

CYCLE HIRE
First Floor, Dolphin Shopping Centre,
Poole. Tel: 01202 680123;
www.cycle-paths.co.uk
FISHING
Poole Sea Angling Centre
Rear of 5 High Street, Poole.
Tel: 01202 676597;
www.pooleseaanglingcentre.co.uk
WATERSPORTS
FC Watersports Academy
by Sandbanks Hotel, Sandbanks, Poole.
Tel: 01202 708283;
www.fcwatersports.co.uk
Rockley Watersports
Rockley Point Sailing Centre,
west of Poole.
Tel: 0870 777 0541;
www.rockleywatersports.com
The Waterboard
14–16 Station Road, Poole.
Tel: 01202 738448;
www.thewaterboard.co.uk
WALKING
Ghost Walks of Old Poole Town
Meet at Scaplen's Court Museum,
Sarum Street.
Tel: 07977 969080

Stour Valley Way
A 64-mile (103km) route between
Christchurch and Stourhead.

ANNUAL EVENTS & CUSTOMS
Bournemouth
Classic Cars on the Prom. Sun from
4pm, mid-Apr to mid-Sep.
Carnival, first week Aug.
Tel: 0771 359 0629;
www.bournemouthcarnival.org.uk
Wimborne
Folk Festival, mid-Jun.
www.wimbornefolkfestival.co.uk
Swanage
Regatta & Carnival Week, late Jul,
early Aug; www.swanagecarnival.com
Tarrant Hinton
Great Dorset Steam Fair, late
Aug–early Sep.
Tel: 01258 488928;
www.gdsf.co.uk

TEA ROOMS

All Fired Up Café
The Square, 35–37 Bourne Avenue,
Bournemouth, BH2 6DT
Tel: 01202 558030
www.allfiredupceramics.co.uk
This is a café with a huge difference
– tuck into herbal, fruit or iced teas,
Italian coffee and tasty home-baked
cakes, while you decorate your own
pottery blank. Your piece will be fully
fired and glazed for you to collect a few
days later.

Blue Pool and Tea House
Furzebrook, near Wareham, BH20 5AT
Tel: 01929 551408
www.bluepooluk.com
The Blue Pool is a beauty spot created
from an old clay works, surrounded
by 25 acres (10ha) of woodland and
heath. The genteel Tea House was
first opened here in 1935 and boasts
its own little museum. Today it serves
cream teas and light lunches, and
is the perfect stopping place for
refreshments as you explore the area.

Worth Café Centre
Worth Matravers,
Swanage, BH19 3LQ
Tel: 01929 439360
In the middle of a row of converted
stone barns, this cosy café offers a
variety of fresh home-made treats
such as Dorset apple cake, as well as
tempting lunches such as spinach and
mushroom bake.

The Courtyard Tea Room
Model Village, The Square,
Corfe Castle, BH20 5EZ
Tel: 01929 481234
Home-cooked food is the order of the
day at this tea room in the middle of
Corfe village. As well as cream teas
and cakes, you can tuck into daily
lunchtime specials. In fine weather,
you can eat out under shady umbrellas
in the 17th-century courtyard.

SWANAGE

The Bankes Arms Hotel
Watery Lane, Studland, BH19 3AU
Tel: 01929 450225

Once the haunt of smugglers, this creeper-clad old inn is renowned for its large menu of fresh fish and seafood, including fresh mussels, crab gratin and lobster dishes. There are meat options, too, such as lamb noisettes in mint, honey and orange sauce. Each year the pub hosts a beer festival, with around 60 real ales on tap accompanied by music, Morris dancing and stone carving in the garden.

The Castle Inn
Main Road, West Lulworth, BH20 5RN
Tel: 01929 400311

Thatched and beamed, this atmospheric old pub close to Lulworth Cove is perfectly placed for walkers and other visitors. There's an extensive tiered garden, which fills up quickly on summer days, and is especially popular with families. Dogs are permitted too. The menu includes some staples such as chicken, ham and mushroom pie, seafood stew, and fillet steak with oysters. And for something unusual, flambé dishes are cooked at your table. Beers include Ringwood Best.

Langton Arms
Tarrant Monkton, DT11 8RX
Tel: 01258 830225
www.thelangtonarms.co.uk

This lovely old thatched pub in the centre of the village has a great reputation for its food, and is popular with families year round. The menu changes frequently, but includes tasty treats such as game pie, delicious baked aubergine with ratatouille and mozzarella, and locally made Purbeck ice cream or maybe profiteroles with butterscotch sauce. There's a good-sized beer garden for fine weather and a children's play area.

New Forest

ASHURST	EXBURY
BEAULIEU	FORDINGBRIDGE
BREAMORE	FRITHAM
BROCKENHURST	LYMINGTON
BUCKLER'S HARD	LYNDHURST
BURLEY	MINSTEAD
CALSHOT	RINGWOOD
CHRISTCHURCH	ROCKBOURNE
ELING	

The New Forest, an ancient Royal hunting forest, was created 'new' by William the Conqueror in 1079 as a preserve for hunting deer. The forest is not all dense woodland, as first-time visitors often expect, but consists largely of heathland, with a rich variety of plant life and animals, including the semi-wild ponies, cattle, donkeys and squirrels. Explore beyond the major tourist spots on foot, by bike or on horseback to discover the magic of the place. There are towns, villages and gardens to visit, and attractions include Beaulieu's famous motor museum and the Solent coast.

Unmissable attractions

Witness the 'wild' New Forest ponies roaming through woodland and grazing freely on the rough grass with their foals...learn to sail at one of Lymington's busy sailing schools...admire the gardens at Exbury House, famous for its bold rhododendron blooms...power along tracks on a mountain bike or take a leisurely horse-drawn wagon ride at Burley...throw in a line and catch a crab on Mudeford's pretty little quayside...stand by the Rufus Stone, the spot where King William II is supposed to have died...bottle-feed a calf or a kid at Longdown Activity Farm...sit quietly in St Nicholas' church at Brockenhurst, the oldest church in the forest...watch fine thoroughbred racehorses galloping across open ground near Roman Rockbourne.

3 Highcliffe Castle
Acquired by the local council in 1977, Highcliffe Castle has undergone much restoration. The first task was to ensure that the structure and roof were secure. Funding from the National Lottery has enabled a renovation programme to take place.

1 Christchurch
The Priory Church has been at the heart of this town for more than 1,200 years, although the present building was begun in the 11th century.

2 Lymington
A leading sailing resort, Lymington has two marinas and is the main port for ferries going to Yarmouth on the Isle of Wight. This lively town with its Georgian and Victorian houses has a great, buzzing atmosphere.

4

4 Cycling in the New Forest
The New Forest Cycle Network links several sites and villages. Most tracks are shared with horse-riders and walkers.

5 Hurst Castle
The castle is one of several defensive southern coast castles erected by Henry VIII. Its low walls were difficult to target from a vessel at sea, and the sturdy structure was able to support heavy artillery.

5

ASHURST

A string of villages lines the A35 between Totton and Lyndhurst. Ashurst, where the housing suddenly stops and the countryside proper begins, was known simply as Lyndhurst Road, like its railway station, until the 1920s, and has developed as prime commuter housing for nearby Southampton. The railway bridge in Ashurst once defined the outer boundary of the New Forest, and this was as close to the hotels and facilities of Lyndhurst that the local landowners would permit the railway to encroach – in fact, the line was forced to take such a circuitous route that it was nicknamed the 'Weymouth Wanderer'. Further on, to the southwest is the popular campsite of Ashurst Woods.

East of Ashurst, Longdown Activity Farm is a hands-on attraction for all ages, including bottle-feeding goat kids, and calves. Close by is the New Forest Otter, Owl and Wildlife Conservation Park

Insight

NEW FOREST PONIES

New Forest ponies may roam freely, but they are not strictly wild – they belong to the commoners. The Victorians 'improved' the hardy ponies that had grazed the forest for centuries, surviving on a diet of gorse, bracken and brambles, by inter-breeding them with Arab stallions – and now they mainly eat grass. Every autumn the ponies are rounded up for branding and marking, and several times a year ponies are sold at Beaulieu Road Station.

– 25 secluded acres (10ha) of ancient woodland where native species are conserved including red squirrels, harvest mice and barn owls.

BEAULIEU

The pretty little village of Beaulieu has become synonymous with the National Motor Museum, the private passion of the enterprising then Lord Montagu. His forefathers acquired the Beaulieu estate in Tudor times, with its Cistercian abbey founded in 1204. The abbey was torn down as part of the dissolution of the monasteries countrywide, but the fine cloisters survived and now contain a re-created monastic garden; the refectory became the parish church; and the Domus, the lay brothers' apartments, now houses an interestng exhibition about abbey life. The Tudor house created from the 14th-century gatehouse was reconstructed in

the 19th century as the present Palace House, and today shows the domestic workings of a Victorian household. During World War II the estate became the top-secret training school for those involved in the Special Operations Executive (SOE), where agents prepared for operations behind enemy lines in occupied France and Europe, and this fascinating story is told in the Secret Army Exhibition.

Lord Montagu first opened this lovely Palace House to the public in 1952, and the brilliant motor museum is dedicated to the memory of his father. It was in fact John Montagu who had successfully petitioned Parliament to abolish the 12mph (19kph) speed limit, among other notable achievements. Today there are more than 250 vintage beauties and stars of the car world to admire in this famous collection, ranging from world record breakers as 'Bluebird' and 'Golden Arrow' to TV favourites, including Mr Bean's green Mini, and James Bond's Lotus

Insight

FLYING BOATS
Before the advent of World War II, the lumbering forms of flying boats were a familiar sight on Southampton Water. They were based at Hythe, a coastal town northeast of Beaulieu, and flew from here to all parts of the British Empire otherwise inaccessible to aircraft. The parent company was Imperial Airways, which was later nationalised as British Overseas Airways Corporation (BOAC).

BEAULIEU RIVER

submarine car from the movie *The Spy Who Loved Me*. A trip on the 'Wheels' pod ride transports you through a century of motoring history, and you can explore the site on a replica 1912 bus or the high-level monorail. Look out for the special events that take place throughout the year.

BREAMORE

Breamore (pronounced 'Bremmer') is a truly ancient village. Stretching across lush water meadows and up the western chalk slopes of the Avon Valley, in the northeast corner of the New Forest. It is one of the area's loveliest villages, with many 17th-century redbrick cottages and farmhouses, mostly thatched, grouped peacefully around a green. It's a scene jealously guarded from change, and even the village stocks still stand, opposite the Bat and Ball pub. The little church, which dates from about 980 AD, is one of the most interesting Saxon survivals in the area. Despite later alterations,

Insight

ROYAL HUNTING GROUND

William the Conqueror created the New Forest as a preserve for deer, regarded from early times as the true sporting beasts of kings. Forest Law was severe and enforced to maintain the best possible environment for the 'beasts of the chase'. Today there are five species of deer in the forest, of which the most numerous are fallow deer. They are managed by the New Forest keepers, employed by the Forestry Commission. Of all the deer in the forest, the white buck, a rare albino form, was the most favoured. Legend has it that Henry VIII and his courtiers once chased a white buck quite a way through the forest towards Ringwood, and that he spared its life at the request of the ladies. Today the 'White Hart' appears on many inn signs.

including a Norman porch and a 14th-century chancel, it still preserves much of the Saxon fabric, notably flints and some Roman bricks in its construction.

The redbrick Elizabethan manor house of Breamore, built on the hillside in 1583, was purchased by Queen Anne's physician Sir Edward Hulse in the 18th century, and is still a family home with collections of paintings, furniture, needlework and porcelain. The Great Hall contains its original carved stone fireplace, and there is a Victorian kitchen with gleaming copperware.

The fascinating Countryside Museum occupies the old farmyard, and has full-size replicas of the village shops that would have made the estate self-sufficient, including a wheelwright's, a blacksmith's and a brewery.

BROCKENHURST

Brockenhurst is a large and very pleasant village set amid the peaceful wooded countryside. On the northern outskirts are two of the largest and loveliest of the New Forest 'lawns', Butts Lawn and Balmer Lawn, the latter overlooked by an elegant hotel.

New Forest churches tend to stand aloof from their villages and ancient Brockenhurst's St Nicholas' church, hidden away to the east, is no exception. It is reputedly the oldest in the forest, and it was the only one recorded in the 1086 Domesday survey. The yew tree that almost smothers the building has a girth of more than 20 feet (6m) and is more than 1,000 years old.

Northwest of Brockenhurst village is Rhinefield Ornamental Drive. It features a variety of coniferous trees, including very large redwoods. Forest walks on either side of the drive include a special 'Tall Trees Walk'. At the bottom of the drive is Rhinefield House Hotel, a flamboyant Jacobean-style house, built in 1890 on the site of a hunting lodge used by Charles II. Magnificent gardens surround the mansion. Further on, Bolderwood Drive passes close to the famous ancient Knightwood Oak, and the deer sanctuary where platforms offer a view of deer roaming the forest.

RHINEFIELD ORNAMENTAL DRIVE

BUCKLER'S HARD

Two redbrick, terraced rows of Georgian houses face each other across a wide open space that slopes gently down to the Beaulieu River, on the Beaulieu estate. The area is kept free of cars and presents a peaceful rural scene today. Yet Buckler's Hard, originally called Montagu Town, was the shipyard that built many of the men-of-war for Nelson's fleet, including *Agamemnon*, Nelson's favourite ship. The yard was immensely busy, but overreached itself and folded in 1811. During World War II Buckler's Hard revived its shipbuilding tradition, and some parts of a Mulberry Harbour for the D-Day landings were constructed here. The Maritime Museum displays models of many of the ships built here, and reconstructed cottage interiors offer an insight into the life of 18th-century shipyard workers.

Today, pleasure craft ride Beaulieu River and, in summer, cruises set off from the quay. A riverside walk leads to Beaulieu.

BURLEY

Burley is an excellent centre for walking, horse-riding and mountain biking. It's also a good place to stop for a cream tea. It is a pretty village set high above the River Avon amid the bleak and gaunt heathlands of the western New Forest, where ponies and cattle roam freely. Burley Beacon is the high point of the village, reached by the gravel track from Pound Lane, and from its height the view expands westwards over the Avon Valley. Even better is the view from Castle Hill, topped by an Iron Age camp, at nearby Burley Street. Red deer roam in the grounds of grand Burley Manor.

During the 1950s Burley had its own resident witch, Sybil Leek, who dressed in black robes with a jackdaw perched on her shoulder. Despite her 'white' tendencies, local resentment caused her to flee to America. Since then the village has specialised in witchcraft shops as well as the usual range of antiques and souvenirs. A window in the little

BURLEY

CALSHOT

church commemorates Constance Applebee, who died in 1981 at the ripe old age of 107. Burley is also home to New Forest Cider, a cider farm with a shop and an exhibition to show how it is made.

CALSHOT

The well-preserved remains of one of Henry VIII's coastal gun-stations, built between 1539 and 1540 against the real threat of a French invasion, stands on a gravel spit jutting out into the Solent. It continued to be of military importance, and today contains a reconstructed barrack room complete with replica 1890s furnishings and a display on the history of the fort. During both world wars it was a Royal Naval Air Station, a base for seaplanes and flying boats, and in the 1920s and 30s the Schneider Trophy seaplane races were held here.

The beach has been designated a coastal country park and adjoins Lepe Country Park to the west, forming a mile-long (1.6km) stretch of shoreline backed by pines and pleasant cliff-top walks. The area is known for its D-Day remains and variety of habitats – shingle beaches, reed beds, marsh and brackish ponds – which attract an extensive range of marine and bird life.

CHRISTCHURCH

This ancient town lies on the south coast where the rivers Stour and Avon pour their waters into the bay. At the time of the Domesday survey there were a mere 21 houses here, and it was then named Twynham. The church was started later in the 11th century, and became an Agustinian priory around 1150. Today all that remains is the Priory Church, which looms gold above the town, and is well worth exploring inside for its carvings in both stone and wood. Look out for the Norman turret in the north transept, and the superb carving of the Salisbury Chantry. Nearby Place Mill, mentioned in the Domesday Book, was used for fulling (cleaning and thickening cloth) and

91

Activity

THE HAMPSHIRE AVON

The River Avon rises to the east of Devizes and flows southwards for 48 miles (77km) to the English Channel at Christchurch. In its upper chalky reaches it is a noted trout stream, but where it flows into Hampshire past Breamore and Fordingbridge the acid soils of the New Forest change its nature and it becomes a river for coarse fishing. Below Ringwood it is renowned for salmon. The waymarked Avon Valley Path follows the river for 34 miles (54.5km) from Salisbury to Christchurch.

corn grinding until 1808, and has displays of old milling items, with an art and crafts gallery upstairs.

One of Christchurch town's most unusual sights is its surviving ducking stool, reached via a flagged alleyway beside the Olde George Inn – a wooden stool on the end of a pole which can be swung out into the chilly millstream, in a scolds' punishment revived with good

humour in 1986. The town's Red House Museum is a collection of local and natural history, housed in an appealing old Georgian house with a lovely garden.

Across the wide estuary, the pastel coloured nostalgic beach huts in rows on Mudeford's sandy peninsula are a cheerful throwback to childhood bucket-and-spade holidays of the early 20th century. This windswept peninsula has an archaeological record dating back 12,500 years, when Stone Age hunter-gatherers left the remains of a campsite on its outer, seaward edge. Some 10,500 years later, Iron Age folk had settled here and built up a good trading port on the inner shore, where Barn Field stands today. The great Double Dikes date from this period, built to shelter a village of timber-framed dwellings.

Barn Field itself has remained untouched by farming improvements since the Romans left in around AD 410 – a rare status jealously protected by conservationists. It's

SOLDIER BROTHERS' MEMORIAL

In Exbury's Church of St Catherine is a fine bronze memorial by Cecil Thomas to John and Alfred Forster, brothers who were killed in World War I. It shows a soldier's effigy lying on a tomb, and is impressively lifelike, down to the folds in the greatcoat and the lacing-up of the boots. The young sculptor was wounded in the war, and while in hospital met and befriended Lt Alfred Forster of the Royal Scots Greys, who later died of his wounds. After the war, Lord and Lady Forster commissioned Thomas to design a memorial to Alfred and his brother.

an area of low, acid grassland gripping onto thin soil over gravel and sand, maintained down the centuries by the salt-laden winds and the sharp teeth of the rabbit population. Decimation of the rabbits in the 1950s by myxomatosis allowed gorse and bramble to gain a hold, but a recent scrub clearance and controlled grazing by cattle, managed by English Nature, has done much to restore the original balance. Today it is an important site for ground-nesting birds such as the skylark and meadow pipit, and adorned with heath bedstraw, autumn hawkbit and harebell.

ELING

The Saxon village of Eling, on a little tidal creek off Southampton Water, was a shipbuilding village until the end of the 19th century. Before that it was a small port from where Henry I is said to have sailed to Normandy in 1130.

The creek, a sheltered little harbour for sailing craft, is crossed by a fast causeway with sluice gates to hold back the high tides and, in the little building on the northern shore, the power of Southampton Water's famous double tides is harnessed and used to produce wholemeal flour. Eling Tide Mill is the only surviving tide mill regularly milling pure stoneground flour. The

Domesday Book of 1086 records a mill here, but the present building dates from the 18th century. It was restored in 1980 and milling demonstrations are given, depending on the tides. You can learn more about Eling and neighbouring Totton in the fascinating heritage centre located by the mill.

The causeway across the creek at Eling carries the only remaining toll road in Hampshire, which has been in operation since at least 1418.

EXBURY

This pleasant estate village nestling on the Beaulieu River is famed for the fine rhododendron gardens at Exbury House. They were the creation of banker Lionel de Rothschild, whose passion was gardening – and he gardened on a magnificent scale.

Rothschild started here in the 1920s, with 600 acres (243ha) of wooded slopes overlooking the peaceful river, which he split into 250 acres (101ha) of gardens and 350 acres (142ha) of arboretum. He imported more than 1,000 varieties of rhododendron, then created 452 more by careful crossing. Today the gardens are run by his son, Edmund. The mild climate of the Beaulieu River valley ensures a long flowering season, with breathtaking displays between April and June. Camellias, azaleas and magnolias contribute a great deal to the glory of an Exbury spring. Other 'gardens' on the site include a daffodil meadow, rock garden, rose garden and water garden. Children may enjoy the miniature steam railway, which offers a 20-minute tour of the Summer Lane Garden, leading to the American Garden. Dogs on a short lead are welcome.

FORDINGBRIDGE

Fordingbride stands at a shallow point on the River Avon, and is the northern gateway of the New Forest.

It grew up around the light industries of pottery, brick-making and canvas sailcloth weaving

97

and dates back to the Domesday survey and beyond. Branksome China, located on Shaftesbury Street, continues the old tradition of porcelain manufacture and hand painting, offering tours and a shop.

The town's elegant 14th-century bridge has seven arches, so solid in their stonework that they were drilled only with great difficulty during World War II by Royal Engineers, who were inserting explosives ready to blow the bridge up in the event of enemy invasion.

Despite the destruction of much of the old town by fire in 1702, there are around 70 listed buildings scattered through Fordingbridge, and a town walk takes you past many of the best. St Mary's Church is notable for the fine 15th-century carved roof in the north chancel chapel, and for its Miracle Stone on the outer wall of the north chapel.

The Fordingbridge Museum includes an exhibition about the artist Augustus John, as well as artefacts to illustrate tales of smuggling in the town and many other curiosities.

South of the town off the A338, at South Gorley, Hockey's Farm is an open-air farming museum, with fossil displays, a deer park, and a farm shop well stocked with home-produced beef and lamb, sausages, cakes and home-cured bacon.

FRITHAM

The isolated rural hamlet of Fritham lies to the north of the A31. The plains to the south were used as an airfield during World War II, and to the north you'll find the lonely settlement, perhaps founded by squatters, known as Nomansland. The village inn, the Royal Oak, is a small traditional country pub, with few frills. Snug under its thatched roof, it is a reminder of a simple age when pigs snuffled in the woods, each home had a cow or two and some hens, services in the tiny tin chapel were held twice on Sundays attended by all, and the main road out was a grassy track.

HERE STOOD
THE OAK TREE,
ON WHICH AN ARROW
SHOT BY
SIR WALTER TYRRELL
AT A STAG,
GLANCED AND STRUCK
KING WILLIAM
THE SECOND,
SURNAMED RUFUS,
ON THE BREAST,
OF WHICH HE
INSTANTLY DIED,
ON THE SECOND
DAY OF AUGUST,
ANNO 1100.

KING WILLIAM
THE SECOND,
SURNAMED RUFUS,
BEING SLAIN
AS BEFORE RELATED
WAS LAID IN A
CART, BELONGING
TO ONE PURKIS,
AND DRAWN FROM
HENCE, TO
WINCHESTER, AND
BURIED IN THE
CATHEDRAL CHURCH
OF THAT CITY.

RUFUS STONE

LYMINGTON

NO MOORING LANDING ONLY

Between 1863 and 1921, Fritham's fortunes changed and the village thrived as the base for a gunpowder factory. The factory made use of local charcoal and water from a chalybeate spring. When the factory closed Fritham returned to a quieter existence.

At Canterton Glen, southeast of Fritham, lies the Rufus Stone, a small memorial marking the place where King William II (known as William Rufus), met his untimely death in 1100. William was a keen huntsman, and was killed by an arrow supposedly intended for a deer. The Rufus Stone is believed to mark the spot where he died, but some believe it was much nearer Bolderwood, or Stoney Cross, or Fritham itself. Some historians also question whether the King's death was really an accident. Whatever the truth, his brother Henry rode straight to Winchester to be proclaimed king, while William's body was carried there on the cart of a charcoal burner.

LYMINGTON

Lymington is a busy sailing town at the mouth of the Lymington River. It received its charter in 1200 and became a free port, flourishing as the closest mainland harbour to the Isle of Wight, to which ferries still run. In the Middle Ages Lymington rivalled Southampton as a major port – and the numerous creeks around here were frequented by smugglers well into the 18th century. Today the tidal salt marshes stretch for 10 miles (16km), and are an important national nature reserve.

For many years the town's prosperity depended on the production of salt, but this trade eventually died out and Lymington briefly became a fashionable bathing place. By the end of the 19th century it had really developed as a sailing centre, and today the town has an excellent yacht basin and is the headquarters of two sailing clubs. There is boat building too and, as with many ports, it is famed for its inns – reputedly there were once 45.

The wide Georgian and Victorian High Street, which climbs the hill from the quay to the church, bursts into life on Saturdays when there is a vibrant 700-year-old market, with a great variety of stalls laid out along both sides of the street. Enjoy the view from the hilltop back down across the river, then take a look at the Church of St Thomas, which looks 18th century, with its jaunty white cupola and galleried interior, but is actually medieval. The town's St Barbe Museum is dedicated to the history of the New Forest coast, including hands-on displays for children, while its art gallery offers an ever-changing range of exhibitions of world-class artworks.

To the north of Lymington is lovely Spinners, a beautiful woodland garden showing rhododendrons, magnolias, Japanese maples and much more. To the south, on Hurst Spit, stands Hurst Castle, one of Henry VIII's defences and part of the modern coastal artillery defences until 1956.

LYNDHURST

The 'Capital of the New Forest' is quite a sizeable town, and is the only one located within the historical confines of the forest. It was formerly designated the New Forest's administrative centre in 1079 by William I, and it continues to be the official seat of the ancient Court of Verderers whose aim is to protect the rights of the commoners. The Court Room and the Forestry Commission offices are both housed in the beautiful 17th-century Queen's House, and the Verderers meet here every two months. All New Forest animals are under their jurisdiction, while the patrolling of the forest is in the hands of four 'Agisters' – a medieval word meaning 'collector'. The Forestry Commission manages the woodland of the New Forest.

Lyndhurst is a town of narrow streets leading off the main High Street, which snarls up with traffic during peak holiday times. It is full of tourist shops and eating places, with Victorian and Edwardian architecture

HURST CASTLE

to admire. The church, on the site of two earlier ones, dominates the High Street with its 160-foot (49m) spire and dates from 1860. It contains windows by Burne-Jones and a fresco, *The Parable of the Virgins*, by Lord Leighton. In the village churchyard lies Mrs Hargreaves, who died in 1934. As the little Alice Liddell, she was the real child that inspired Lewis Caroll's *Alice in Wonderland*. The town is also the home of the important New Forest Visitor Centre and Museum.

Lyndhurst's central position makes it an ideal base for exploring the forest which still presses up close to the town's boundaries,. To the west of Lyndhurst is the picturesque thatched hamlet of Swan Green, formerly the site of an important pony fair, and Emery Down, famed for its Portuguese fireplace, which stands alone in the open air. It was constructed of cobble stones on the site of a building that was occupied by Portuguese troops during World War I, and serves as a memorial to them. The New Forest Reptile Centre, a conservation and education centre dedicated to rare native species, is near by. To the east is Bolton's Bench, a starting point for walks over White Moor Heath.

In summer an open-topped City Sightseeing bus, with space for bicycles, runs every hour from Lyndhurst, and makes 13 stops, including Lymington and Beaulieu.

MINSTEAD

Minstead is a picturesque village and consists of small clusters of cottages amidst trees and pastures and set around an inn and the church. The latter is of curious construction, having the outward appearance of an old house, all gables and dormers. This is the result of successive 'updates' by local builders who had little idea of ecclesiastical construction, reflecting the days when the forest locals knew little of the world beyond. The interior has rows of box pews and a plethora of galleries. Sir

Arthur Conan Doyle (1867–1930), whose most famous literary creation was the detective Sherlock Holmes, lies buried here.

To the northwest of the village lies Furzey Gardens, renowned among many botanists and horticulturalists, comprising 8 acres (3ha) of informal planting, which includes azaleas, rhododendrons, ferns, heathers and Chilean fire trees. Within the garden are a thatched Tudor cottage, a crafts gallery and an art gallery.

RINGWOOD

Ringwood is a venerable market town on the River Avon, and anglers come from miles around for the coarse and salmon fishing of this reach. This busy centre has always been the New Forest's market town, with its modern buildings blending well with the Georgian houses and older cottages.

There is a good modern shopping centre, and the attractive High Street has traditional shops including fishing tackle suppliers and a gunsmith. The Ringwood Brewery has an outlet on Christchurch Road. In West Street stands Monmouth House, where the Duke of Monmouth was held prisoner after his defeat at Sedgemoor in 1685, before being sent to London for execution.

Learn more about the history of the area at the Ringwood Town & Country Experience, a heritage centre to the north of the A31, with reconstructed Victorian shop interiors, a fabulous carousel, and one of the bouncing bombs, developed nearby for the RAF 'Dambusters' in World War II. The Moors Valley Country Park at Ashley Heath offers walks and cycle trails, and other attractions, including a narrow-guage steam railway.

To the south of Ringwood, at Crow, is Liberty's Raptor and Reptile Centre. There are lots of birds of prey, including eagles, hawks, owls and vultures and reptiles such as giant tortoises, snakes and lizards.

MOORS VALLEY

ROCKBOURNE

The village of Rockbourne, on the high chalklands northwest of Fordingbridge, is one of Hampshire's prettiest villages, with thatched cottages dating back to Tudor and Georgian times nestling beside a stream in a valley bottom.

On the downs above are the remains of three barrows: Grans, Knapp and Duck's Nest Long Barrow. However, Rockbourne's real fame rests on the Roman villa discovered to the south of the village by a farmer in 1942, when he was digging out a ferret. The villa was a large courtyard type of mansion, possibly part of an imperial estate, with more than 70 rooms, several bath suites, farm houses and work-shops. It was occupied from the mid-2nd century AD until the collapse of Roman rule in the early 5th century. Although much of it has been excavated it has to some extent been backfilled for its own protection, since the site is not under cover, but several mosaics may be seen.

As well as the villa, there was a settlement and a probable cattle enclosure on Rockbourne Down, while nearby Bokerley Dyke, a late-Roman earthwork, acts as a local boundary. The museum has excellent display of pottery, jewellery and elaborate iron work, a large coin hoard and two Roman milestones. Found in the fabric of the villa, where they had been re-used as building material, the milestones date from the reigns of Trajan Decius (AD 249–51) and Tetricus II (AD 272).

Insight

HORSE FLESH

To the northeast of Rockbourne lies the peaceful village of Whitsbury. It is home to the Whitsbury Manor Stud, one of the most successful horse breeding, training and racing stables in Britain. The open downland surrounding the village provides an ideal training ground for potential winners. Racehorses Desert Orchid and Rhyme and Reason were both bred here.

TOURIST INFORMATION CENTRES

Christchurch
49 High Street.
Tel: 01202 471780;
www.christchurchtourism.info

Fordingbridge
Kings Yard, Salisbury Street.
Tel: 01425 654560;
www.visitfordingbridge.com

Lyndhurst
New Forest Visitor Information Centre,
Main Car Park.
Tel: 023 8028 2269;
www.thenewforest.co.uk

PLACES OF INTEREST

Apple Court Garden & Nursery
Hordle Lane, Hordle, Lymington.
Tel: 01590 642130;
www.applecourt.com

**Beaulieu: National Motor Museum,
Palace House, Beaulieu Abbey**
Tel: 01590 612123;
www.beaulieu.co.uk

Bolderwood Deer Platform
Signed from Bolderwood car park.
Fallow deer fed here.
www.forestry.gov.uk/newforest

Branksome China
Fordingbridge.
Tel: 01425 652010;
www.branksomechina.co.uk

Breamore Manor House
& Countryside Museum
Tel: 01725 512468;
www.breamorehouse.com

Buckler's Hard
Tel: 01590 616203;
www.bucklershard.co.uk

Calshot Fort (EH)
Tel: 02380 892023

Christchurch Priory Church
Quay Road, Christchurch.
Tel: 01202 485804;
www.christchrchpriory.org

Eling Tide Mill
The Toll Bridge, Eling, Totton.
Tel: 023 8086 9575;
www.elingtidemill.org.uk

Exbury Gardens & Steam Railway
Near Beaulieu.
Tel: 023 8089 1203; www.exbury.co.uk

Fordingbridge Museum
King's Yard, Fordingbridge.
Tel: 01425 655222;
www.fordingbridgemuseum.co.uk

Furzey Gardens
Minstead. Tel: 023 8081 2464;
www.furzey-gardens.org

Hockey's Farm
South Gorley.
Tel: 01425 652542.

Hurst Castle
Hurst Point, by Keyhaven.
Tel: 01590 642344 or 01590 642500;
www.hurst-castle.co.uk

Moors Valley Country Park
Ashley Heath, Ringwood.
Tel: 01425 470721

New Forest Cider
Littlemead, Pound Lane, Burley.
Tel: 01425 403589;
www.newforestcider.co.uk

New Forest Museum
Main car park, High street, Lyndhurst.
Tel: 023 8028 3444;
www.newforestmuseum.org.uk

New Forest Reptile Centre
Emery Down. Tel: 023 8028 3141;
www.forestry.gov.uk/newforest

Place Mill
Quay Road, Christchurch.
Tel: 01202 487626;
www.visitchristchurch.info

Red House Museum
Quay Road, Christchurch.
Tel: 01202 482860

Ringwood Brewery Store
138 Christchurch Road, Ringwood.
Tel: 01425 471177;
www.ringwoodbrewery.co.uk

Rockbourne Roman Villa
Tel: 01725 518541; www.hants.gov.
uk/museum/rockbourne

St Barbe Museum and Art Gallery
New Street, Lymington.
Tel: 01590 676969;
www.stbarbe-museum.org.uk

Sammy Miller Motorcycle Museum & Farm Trust
New Milton. Tel: 01425 620777;
www.sammymiller.co.uk

Spinners Garden & Nursery
Boldre, by Lymington.
Tel: 01590 673347

FOR CHILDREN

Burley Park Deer Safari
Burley Park, Burley.
Tel: 07801 345264;
www.newforestsafari.co.uk

Liberty's Raptor and Reptile Centre
Crow Lane, Crow.
Tel: 01425 476487;
www.libertyscentre.co.uk

Longdown Activity Farm
South of A35, near Ashurst.
Tel: 023 8029 3326;
www.longdownfarm.co.uk

New Forest Otter, Owl and Wildlife Conservation Park
Longdown, near Ashurst.
Tel: 023 8029 2408;
www.ottersandowls.co.uk

Paultons Park
Ower, near Romsey.
Tel: 023 8081 4455;
www.paultonspark.co.uk

SHOPPING

Farmers' Markets
Held in towns throughout the New Forest. Markets take place on alternate Sundays in Beaulieu, Lymington, Lyndhurst and Fordingbridge.
Tel: 023 8028 5185;
 www.forestfriendlyfarming.org.uk.

Christchurch Market
High Street, every Mon.

Lyburn Farmhouse Cheesemakers
Lyburn Farm, Landford, Wiltshire.
Tel: 01794 390451;
www.lyburncheese.co.uk

SPORTS & ACTIVITIES

Go Ape!
Moors Valley Country Park, Horton Road, Ashley Heath.
Tel: 0870 458 9063; www.goape.co.uk
High-wire forest adventure.

BOATING

Beaulieu River cruises
From Buckler's Hard, 3 miles (4.5km) south of Beaulieu.
Liquid Logistics
Tel: 01590 624730;
www.liquidlogistics.co.uk

CANOEING AND KAYAKING.

Mudeford Ferry Adventure Voyages
Mudeford Quay.
Tel: 01202 488662;
www.adventurevoyages.co.uk

CYCLE HIRE

AA Bike Hire
Fernglen, Gosport Lane, Lyndhurst.
Tel: 023 8028 3349;
 www.aabikehirenewforest.co.uk

Country Lanes Cycle Centre
The Railway Station, Brockenhurst.
Tel: 01590 622627;
www.countrylanes.co.uk
Cycle Xperience Bike Hire
Island Shop, 2–4 Brookly Road,
Brockenhurst.
Tel: 01590 624204;
www.cyclex.co.uk
Forest Leisure Cycling (FLC)
Burley.
Tel: 01425 403584;
www.forestleisurecycling.co.uk
FISHING
Orchard Lakes
New Lane Orchard, New Lane, Bashley,
New Milton.
Tel: 01425 612404
Carp, tench, chub, bream, roach
and rudd.
Everton Grange Lake
Braxton Farm, Lymore Lane,
Milford-on-Sea, Lymington.
Tel: 01590 644499
Carp, chub and tench.

HORSE-RIDING
Burley-Villa School of Riding
Bashley Common Road,
New Milton.
Tel: 01425 610278;
www.burleyvilla.co.uk
WALKING
Avon Valley Path
A 34-mile (51km) path from
Christchurch to Salisbury Cathedral.
Castleman Trailway.
A 16-mile (24km) trail between Upton
and Ringwood.

ANNUAL EVENTS & CUSTOMS
Beaulieu
Boat Jumble, Apr.
Auto Jumble, Sep.
Fireworks, end Oct.
Brockenhurst
New Forest Show, last week Jul at New
Park; www.newforestshow.co.uk
Mudeford
Lifeboat Funday, end Jul on Mudeford
Quay.

TEA ROOMS

The Buttery
19–20 High Street,
Lymington, SO41 9AD
Tel: 01590 672870
www.thebuttery.org
A well-established and deservedly
popular restaurant and tea room,
the Buttery serves speciality coffees
and teas, clotted cream teas, and a
great selection of tasty cakes – all
handmade on the premises. You can
also get light lunches here, and even a
full English breakfast.

The Buttery at the Brock & Bruin
25 Brookley Road,
Brockenhurst, SO42 7RB
Tel: 01590 622958
Home-made cakes and cream teas are
top treats at this restaurant and tea
room. Light lunches are also served
daily, and breakfast too – handy if
you're camping.

Montagu Arms Hotel
Palace Lane,
Beaulieu, SO42 7ZL
Tel: 01590 612324
www.montaguarmshotel.co.uk
An hospitable, 16th-century inn
nestling in the pretty hamlet of
Beaulieu, the Montagu Arms offers
finger sandwiches, loaf cakes, scones,
cream-tea fancies and shortbread.
In season, you can enjoy locally
grown strawberries served with your
afternoon tea.

Tasty Pastries Bakery and Tea Room
16A High Street,
Lyndhurst, SO43 7BD
Tel: 023 8028 3448
The perfect place to pause for tea
and cakes, or perhaps to buy freshly
baked pasties, filled baguettes and
sandwiches for a picnic.

LOCAL
NEW FOREST
SCRUMPY
CIDER

BURLEY

The East End Arms

Main Road, East End,
near Lymington, SO41 5SY
Tel: 01590 626223
www.eastendarms.co.uk

A traditional New Forest pub serving brasserie-style food in the lounge bar, such as Toulouse sausages and toasted goats' cheese baguettes. No food served Monday, or Sunday evening, or early March and October.

The Filly Inn

Lymington Road, Setley,
Brockenhurst, SO42 7UF
Tel: 01590 623449
www.fillyinn.co.uk

The bar snacks at this cosy, traditional pub include baguettes and jacket potatoes, and there is a wider menu offering home-baked pies and perhaps roast ribs in barbecue sauce. There is also an extensive Hindi vegetarian menu, and cream teas are offered in summer. Children are welcome, and dogs permitted too.

The Master Builders House Hotel

Buckler's Hard, SO42 7XB
Tel: 01590 616297
www.themasterbuilders.co.uk

Grassy areas in front of the pub run down to the Beaulieu River, making it a popular spot, especially on summer days. Fish pie and beef bourguignon may appear on the menu, with a good range of light snacks. Beers include Greene King IPA.

The Rose & Thistle

Rockbourne, SP6 3NL
Tel: 01725 518236
www.roseandthistle.co.uk

This postcard-perfect thatched and whitewashed pub has a rose arch and flowers blooming around the door. Fresh food is cooked to order, from Welsh rarebit and roast beef ploughman's to smoked salmon tagliatelle. There is more substantial fare on the evening menu, such as venison steak with chestnut sauce. Beers include Adnams Broadside and Wadworth 6X.

Isle of Wight

INTRODUCTION

The Isle of Wight is the largest island off England's coast. It is separated from the mainland by the Solent and for many years was isolated and forgotten, until popularised in the mid-19th century by the arrival of Queen Victoria and Prince Albert, who built Osborne House here. This is an island of contrasts: the north facing the mainland; the southwest, including the famous Needles battered by Channel storms; and the southeast basking in a subtropical climate. The Isle of Wight has a timeless, old-fashioned appeal, which lingers on, born of its long separation from the mainland.

HOT SPOTS

Unmissable attractions

Join the thousands of boat enthusiasts at Cowes during the island's world-famous sailing regatta held in August...photograph Godshill's chocolate-box pretty, stone and thatched cottages...walk the 15th-century ramparts of Carisbrooke Castle...soak up the atmosphere at Osborne House, Queen Victoria's favourite residence and place of her death...enjoy the traditional seaside amusements and attractions at Sandown...admire panoramic views of the bay and the quintessentially English beach huts that stand guard on the beach at Shanklin...explore Ventnor, which was famous in the 19th century for its alleged curative waters and still popular with holiday-makers...visit 13th-century Calbourne Mill, still in use today.

2

1 Cowes

The town is the scene of the annual Cowes Week regatta when the marina bustles with expensive yachts, sailors and sightseers.

2 Carisbrooke Castle

This impressive 11th-century castle has had a long and varied history but is most well known as a place of imprisonment for Charles I.

3 Freshwater Bay
Popular with walkers, the cove here was well known to Alfred, Lord Tennyson, whose house above the cliffs looked out to sea.

4 Shanklin Chine
Shanklin's precious habitats are home to more than 150 varieties of plants. You will see many of them on a walk through the chine.

5 The Needles

On the hill above the Needles is the 19th-century Needles Battery. The battery formed a part of the coastal defences during both world wars.

5

ALUM BAY

The soaring, spikey chalk outcrops of the Needles are the Isle of Wight's most famous landmark, stretching out to the west and clearly visible from the Dorset coast. Standing around 500 feet (150m) high, they sport a red-and-white striped lighthouse, topped by a helicopter landing platform, which is best seen via boat trips from Alum Bay.

Set at right angles to the chalk, the cliffs at Alum Bay produce the island's most unusual souvenirs: a range of clear glass novelty items that display the distinctive 12 shades of sand. The colours range from pink and gold to orange and brown, and are all found naturally in the cliffs here. If you're feeling artistic, you can even design your own memento at the Alum Bay Sand Shop, within the Needles Park complex.

The sandstone strata of the cliffs are vertical, and were formed some 50 million years ago. You can view them from a spectacular chairlift ride down the cliffs to the beach.

On the cliff edge is a monument to the noted Italian physicist and inventor, Marconi, who set up a wireless and telegraph station here at the end of the 19th century.

The Needles Old Battery at Totland is a gun battery and fort with wonderful views over the Needles to the Dorset coast. It was built in 1863 as part of the defences for the

Activity

THE TENNYSON TRAIL

This 14-mile (21km) trail starts from Carisbrooke and heads southwest up on to Bowcombe Down, then west past many prehistoric tumuli, and into Brighstone Forest, with views over Brighstone Bay. It then heads back up and over onto Mottistone Down and Brook Down before a long descent past the golf course on Afton Down into Freshwater Bay, where it follows the coast path above the cliff. This is Tennyson Down, with a 38-foot (11.5m) monument to the poet at the high point. The path then drops into Alum Bay.

large naval base at Portsmouth. Exhibitions tell the story of the fort during the two world wars, and the headland's past as a secret base for rocket testing. Note that access is on foot, and it's a 15-minute walk across the downs from the Alum Bay car park.

BEMBRIDGE

Bembridge, on the Isle of Wight's eastern tip, was a remote little fishing village in a sheltered haven leading to Brading Quay until the Victorian company, Brading Harbour Improvement and Railway Company set out to reclaim the upper reaches of the haven. They created a deep-water port here, building an embankment between Bembridge and St Helens in 1878 to carry both road and rail. But Bembridge's days as a port were already numbered, and the ferry service to the mainland lasted only until 1888, because the new harbour suffered from silting, although the railway survived until the 20th century.

Today Bembridge is a popular sailing centre and a quiet resort with pleasant walks inland over the reclaimed haven, now marshy meadows, to Brading. At Bembridge Point is the famous Pilot Boat Inn, built in the shape of a boat, and the lifeboat station near by houses displays on its unsinkable craft.

Bembridge Down is crowned by Fort Bembridge (1862–67), the main Victorian fort for the southern Isle of Wight, and offshore, four forts are still visible – the interesting remains of the Victorian defences for Spithead. Bembridge Windmill, half a mile (800m) to the south, dates from 1700 and has its original wooden machinery.

BRADING

In Roman times Bembridge Down was a separate island and Brading faced it across a tidal channel. In about AD 300 the Romans built a villa here, one of the best in Britain with fabulous mosaics, and it remained occupied until the 5th century.

BEMBRIDGE

Nowadays a vineyard clothes the slopes near the villa, continuing a tradition begun in Roman times. In 1338 an embankment was built at Yar Bridge, creating a harbour in order to connect Bembridge Down with the rest of the Isle of Wight. Brading became an important port, but the harbour here, too, suffered from increased silting. It was reclaimed in 1878–80 and is now an area of marshy meadows, a favourite breeding ground for birds.

The town's 'Brading the Experience' illustrates in waxworks the famous and infamous characters who populated 2,000 years of Isle of Wight history, as well as displays of wax animals, a fine collection of steam and vintage cars, and a colourful, carousel-themed café. Brading also has the Lilliput Museum of Antique Dolls and Toys. Morton Manor, rebuilt in 1680, claims to possess the island's most beautiful gardens and has a small vineyard producing a range of the island's best wines. The Church of

St Mary, the oldest church on the island, is believed to mark the spot where St Wilfred converted the Isle of Wight to Christianity, and a chapel contains tombs of the Oglander family, important in affairs of the island for 800 years.

To the northwest of Brading is Nunwell House, a 17th-century mansion and seat of the Oglanders from the Norman conquest until 1980. Charles I spent his last night on the island here.

CALBOURNE

Calbourne is tucked under the downs in the west of the island, an unspoiled little place with a village green, a Norman and a 13th-century church, and pretty stone cottages. The best of these are in Barrington Row, and these low thatched cottages at the back of the village face the diminutive Caul Burn. The stream once powered five watermills. The last surviving, Calbourne Mill, first mentioned in 1299, is still in working order,

135

CARISBROOKE CASTLE

and there is an attached rural life museum interesting old appliances. West of Calbourne, Chessell Pottery is housed in a large old barn. To the east is historic Swainstone House, now a hotel, renovated after being burnt out in an air raid in 1941. It was named after Swein, the 8th- to 9th-century Danish leader, and later belonged to the Bishop of Winchester. The attached 13th-century chapel survived intact.

To the south of Calbourne, Mottistone Manor Garden is known for its herbaceous borders and grassy terraces, planted with fruit trees. There are lots of walking trails through the surrounding estate.

CARISBROOKE

Carisbrooke, once the capital of the island, is inland above the Medina River to the west of Newport, and is overlooked by its castle, one of England's most impressive. The High Street is pleasant, and narrow Castle Street leads up from an old ford and a streamside footpath to the castle.

St Mary's Church, with its lofty 15th-century tower, was the church of a priory dissolved as long ago as 1415.

Carisbrooke Castle is a large, well-preserved Norman fortress built high on an artificial mound. The oldest parts are the keep and the surviving sections of curtain walls, which were constructed in the 12th century and strengthened at the end of the 16th century. The castle is probably best known for its most famous prisoner, Charles I, who sought refuge here but was imprisoned by the Governor until 1648 when he was taken to London for trial and execution.

A head for heights is needed to walk the ramparts, but you will be rewarded with views of the interior of the castle and the surrounding countryside. A great attraction is the well, 161 feet (49m) deep, with a 16th-century wheel to draw up the water in buckets. It is worked today by donkeys – learn more at the Donkey Centre. The castle also houses the Isle of Wight Museum.

COWES

Cowes, on the island's northern tip, is divided by the River Medina. On the west bank is the sailing capital of Britain, on the east is a residential and industrial area, where high-speed ships, flying boats and seaplanes were built during World War II, and the Hovercraft was developed. Beyond all this lies the tranquillity of Osborne House, Queen Victoria's favourite residence.

West Cowes, home of the Royal Yacht Squadron, has an attractive winding High Street and a good array of shops. You can see ships and boats of all sorts from the Victoria Parade. The inaugural Cowes Regatta took place between naval vessels in 1776, and the yacht club was founded in 1815. In 1856 Cowes Castle became the Squadron's headquarters, and the 22 brass guns from the Royal Adelaide, King William IV's yacht, were positioned in front of the castle to start races and salute victorious yachts – as they still do. There have always been Royal yachtsmen – including Edward VII, George IV, George V, Prince Philip and Prince Edward – and during Cowes Week in August the little town is alive with the great and the good of the yachting fraternity.

Cowes has a Maritime Museum, a military history museum, and the Sir Max Aitken Museum, which has a display of nautical instruments, paintings and artefacts.

FRESHWATER

The southwest tip of the island which ends in the jagged chalk pinnacles of The Needles is known as the Freshwater Peninsula. Freshwater village itself is large and bustling, and was made famous by Alfred, Lord Tennyson who came to reside at Farringford – now a hotel – in 1853, soon after he was proclaimed Poet Laureate. He lived there until 1867 when inquisitive visitors, wishing to see the famous man as he walked on the down in cloak and broad-brimmed hat, drove him to his refuge on the Surrey/Sussex border.

FRESHWATER BAY

Insight

RUINED SHELL

Appuldurcombe House, once Hampshire's finest English baroque building, is now a ruined shell, standing in wooded country to the south amid beautiful grounds landscaped by 'Capability' Brown. The mansion was built in 1710 for Sir Robert Worsley, who is commemorated with an obelisk on the nearby down. The house has been uninhabitable since it was bombed, in 1943, during World War II.

Freshwater has now spread south down the western Yar valley towards Freshwater Bay. The famous portrait photographer Julia Margaret Cameron settled here in the 1860s, and her home, Dimbola Lodge, on Terrace Lane, is now a museum to her work.

GODSHILL

Nestling prettily beneath its beautiful 15th-century church tower, this little village of stone-built, thatched cottages is the most visited and photographed place on the island. Attractions include the interesting model of Godshill village and the Nostalgia Toy Museum, and the Old Smithy and Gardens. Godshill is very popular, so come early in the morning to avoid the coaches and the crowds or in the evening after they have gone.

However, one peaceful haven here is the lovely church, which is almost 1,000 years old and contains a rare medieval wall painting, a painting of Daniel in the lions' den (attributed to Rubens), and some monuments to the Worsley family of Appuldurcombe. The nearby Owl and Falconry Centre offers thrilling flying displays, guaranteed to enthrall.

NEWPORT

Newport, the capital of the Isle of Wight, is a venerable old market town on the River Medina. Its squares and narrow, twisting streets may hide the river from the view of the cursory visitor but boats still

GODSHILL

ply their trade at the rejuvenated quay. Here, too, you'll find the arts centre, housed in a large converted warehouse. The pleasant High Street has many attractive buildings, and is dominated by the Guildhall, with its fine Ionic portico market designed by John Nash, now home to the Museum of Island History. St Thomas' Church has a beautiful marble monument designed by Marochetti to Princess Elizabeth, the youngest daughter of Charles I, who died of a fever aged 14 while she was a prisoner in Carisbrooke Castle.

The town was founded in medieval times as the 'new port' for the old capital, Carisbrooke, yet, similarly to Carisbrooke, it can claim to have its roots in Roman times, since a Roman villa, dating from the 3rd century AD, was discovered here in 1926. The villa has been excavated and is now open to the public. Three of the public rooms have tessellated floors, and the largest also has a fireplace – this was an unusual feature in a Roman house. Horticulturists will enjoy the reconstructed Roman herb garden.

Just to the northwest of the town is Parkhurst Prison and further on you'll find Parkhurst Forest, the remaining glades and woodlands of a former royal hunting forest. This ancient woodland has been threaded by waymarked paths and is now one of the last remaining refuges of the red squirrel.

NEWTOWN

Newtown was originally founded in the 13th century on the island's northwest coast, and its grid-iron pattern can be recognised even today. Its large natural harbour was reputed to have anchorage for 50 ships, but continual silting reduced its size and this, coupled with raids by the French, led to the town's decline. Today the little 17th-century Town Hall is in the care of the National Trust, and the harbour is now a nature reserve, echoing to the piping of the curlew and the harsh cry of wild geese.

Insight

OSBORNE HOUSE

During World War I, Osborne House became a convalescent home for officers. Among the men who came here were A A Milne, (creator of Winnie the Pooh), and Robert Graves, who recalled staying here in his memoir, *Goodbye to All That* (1929).

At the head of one of the creeks is Shalfleet, where you can explore the old harbour, heading down to the quay, busy with pleasure craft. Shalfleet's Church of St Michael was saved in a small-scale replay of the saving of Winchester Cathedral. When its stout Norman tower was found to be standing in 10 feet (3m) of clay and water and in danger of collapsing, the foundations were relaid in concrete.

OSBORNE HOUSE

Osborne House, overlooking the Solent to the east of Cowes, was designed as a royal country retreat by Prince Albert and Thomas Cubitt in the fashionable style of a Neapolitan villa, complete with stylish Italianate campaniles and a loggia. Started in 1845, it served both as a family home and for state functions, and this duality is reflected in the mix of homely and grand interiors on display today. Private rooms include the sitting room where the Queen and her consort worked together. Grander, state rooms include the Durbar Room, which has an Indian-style plasterwork ceiling, where an impressive selection of Indian gifts presented to Victoria, Empress of India, are displayed.

Outside are terraced gardens and a walled fruit and flower garden. In the grounds is the lovely Swiss Cottage, a child-size royal playhouse, charmingly furnished in miniature. The playhouse had a serious purpose, too: the royal princes learned about carpentry here, the princesses learned how to cook and manage a household,

OSBORNE HOUSE

and each child had a garden plot in which to grow some vegetables and flowers. A museum next door shows mementoes collected by the Queen's children and grandchildren.

Victoria and Albert loved to walk in the woods at Osborne, and the Prince added to these extensively, planting every sort of British tree. The Queen recorded lovingly in her memoirs that nightingales were frequently to be heard.

THE AUSTRALIAN CONNECTION
In the days when convicts were transported to Australia, most of them left Britain from ships moored off Ryde – the last they ever saw of 'the old country'. Because of this there remains a special connection between the town and Australia. St Thomas' Church is now a heritage centre with an exhibition commemorating the first ships that carried prisoners to Australia, as well as displays of other local history.

Queen Victoria died at Osborne House, in 1901, and her successor Edward VII presented the well-loved mansion to the nation.

Nearby Barton is a much older place, with a medieval manor house rebuilt by Prince Albert as an experimental farm. Today its gardens are open to the public, along with an award-winning vineyard.

RYDE
When island visitors disembark at Ryde from the Portsmouth ferry, ex-London Transport underground trains take them down the 0.5-mile (800m) long pier, necessary because the coast shelves so gently that vessels can get no closer.

Ryde was developed in the late 18th century and is the largest town on the island, with some 24,000 residents. It has a 5-mile (8km) long sandy beach. From the promenade there are views across Spithead and three of the Solent's Victorian forts. Ryde's summer carnival is spectacular and not to be missed.

Insight

THE LOSS OF THE EURIDICE

In 1878 a fine, fully rigged sailing frigate sank off Dunnose Head, south of Shanklin, with the loss of 300 souls. The *Euridice* was a Royal Navy training ship, on her way to Bermuda with a full complement of passengers and crew. It was March and the weather was terrible, but sheltered in the lee of the cliffs, the ship sailed on in ignorance of the true conditions, its portholes open to ventilate the two decks. As she rounded the point and the true storm hit, she took on water and sank in the freezing waters.

Southwest of Ryde is Brickfields Horse Country, with horses of all sizes, wagon rides and pig-racing. At Ashey, Rosemary Vineyard, the largest of the island's three vineyards, offers tours, tastings and a shop. At Fishbourne, to the west, is Quarr Abbey, a modern foundation (1907–14) of Benedictine monks near the ruins of the earlier Cistercian Abbey. The Isle of Wight Steam Railway puffs out of Smallbrook Junction, just south of Ryde on its journey past Havenstreet to Wootton.

SANDOWN & SHANKLIN

The honky-tonk seaside neighbour of more sedate Shanklin, Sandown was founded as a resort in about 1800 and faces southeastwards out to sea across Sandown Bay. It is built at beach level, with the immense chalk walls of Culver Cliff to the north and the cliffed coast of Shanklin and Luccombe to the south. Sandown is a popular venue for family holidays, with its 6 miles (9.6km) of sandy beach, an esplanade and amusement park, a pier of 1878, cinema, zoo specialising in tigers and lemurs, and the fascinating Dinosaur Isle, a museum displaying life-size dinosaurs and offering guided fossil walks. At the Garlic Farm, near Newchurch, you can buy and learn more.

Shanklin, the quieter neighbour to the south, is a resort that

developed with the coming of the railway in 1891, and now has the best collection of beach huts on the island. You reach the beach by a lift from the clifftop, which has a superb view around Sandown Bay to the gleaming white heights of Culver Cliff. Inland is Shanklin Old Village, a former fishing village close to the winding glen of Shanklin Chine. This 300-feet (91.5m) deep, wooded and ferny fissure was much beloved of earlier tourists, including the poet, John Keats, who stayed at the Old Village in 1819 and composed part of *Endymion* here. The Victorians flocked to tread its winding path past the 40-foot (12m) waterfall to the beach. Today, Shanklin Chine still pulls the crowds – its rare flora is of great interest – and the resort also has two theatres and amusements.

SEAVIEW

This family holiday resort to the east of Ryde is renowned for its gently sloping, firm, sandy beach, from which there is safe bathing.

The town still basks in 19th-century charm, with narrow streets lined with villas and shops sloping down to the sea, the peace maintained by the lack of a main through road. Saltern Cottages are a reminder of the old salt industry which thrived here on the bleak marshes in the days before Seaview became a select resort for those who shun the bustle and gaiety of Ryde. To the northwest is the famous Seaview Wildlife Encounter (formerly Flamingo Park), a bird sanctuary where flamingos, peacocks and waterfowl wander freely over green lawns.

VENTNOR

This south coast resort climbs the sheer cliff beneath flat St Boniface Down (the highest point on the island), as a series of terraces behind the sandy beach, so that the mainly Victorian buildings are built-up in layers and are joined by steep zig-zagging roads with corkscrew turns. There is something Mediterranean in this arrangement,

VENTNOR

and Ventnor has been dubbed 'the English Madeira'. Also, the climate, too, is very good. Protected by the bulk of St Boniface Down, it basks in subtropical conditions.

Ventnor was a small fishing village up until 1841 – albeit much involved in smuggling – but in that year, a famous doctor, Sir James Clarke, publicly sang its praises and visitors started to come. The railway arrived in 1866, meaning Ventnor's development as a health resort was assured, attracting, among others, authors Macaulay, Dickens and Thackeray. Later it was the site of the Royal National Hospital for Consumption and Diseases of the Chest. The town's history is explained in the Heritage Museum.

Ventnor divides into two distinct parts, the elegant 'town' on the cliff face, where Ventnor ales are still brewed, and the seaside resort at the foot of the cliff.

The extraordinary climate is manifest in the Ventnor Botanic Gardens, planted in the 1970s, where some 3,500 species include palms and cork trees. The interesting Smuggling Museum, hidden in subterranean caverns beneath the Botanic Garden, has a large collection of fascinating relics, vividly illustrating the days when Ventnor was the unofficial 'headquarters' of illicit trade. Near by is the ancient village of St Lawrence with the Rare Breeds and Waterfowl Park. Isle of Wight Glass, founded in 1973, produces an exciting range of award-winning glassware.

The southern coast between Ventnor and St Catherine's Point is a region of landslides, where great masses of sandstone rock have been, and continue to be, carried down into the sea on a lubricating layer of blue clay. In fact, Ventnor has the biggest urban landslide problem in Britain. The Undercliff, a ledge which extends along the cliffs, is actually the top of an ancient landslide block. To appreciate the coast to the full, walk part of the coastal path between Shanklin and

VENTNOR

Blackgang. From Shanklin the path first lies close to, and then on, the shore until Ventnor and beyond. At St Lawrence, the path climbs up beyond the road and affords good views to the south before reaching Blackgang. Nature lovers will find that the tumbled land of hummocks and hollows with temporary ponds are the first landfall for migratory butterflies, such as the painted lady and clouded yellow. It is also one of the best places to watch migrating birds in spring.

Near by Blackgang Chine there is an extraordinary theme park that combines static displays with fast fairground rides and lovely gardens. In fact the gardens were the initial inspiration for the park, created to attract Victorian vacationers.

YARMOUTH

The Lymington–Yarmouth ferry is the picturesque way of entry to the Isle of Wight, for Yarmouth is a compact little town with narrow streets and attractive houses, and

a small harbour busy with yachts and a flourishing boatbuilder's yard. During the Middle Ages it was the most important Isle of Wight town, but decline set in and by 1800 it had only a few hundred inhabitants.

Yarmouth's sturdy castle was built against the French in 1547 by Henry VIII, and it remained in use until the 1870s. It is hidden down an alley by the ferry, on King's Land, and is easy to miss.

The pier near the lifeboat station was built in 1876 and was originally the landing stage for the Lymington ferry, but now it is a fine walkway.

Yarmouth's church, rebuilt 1614–26, contains an intriguing monument to Sir Robert Holmes, Governor of the Isle of Wight during the reign of Charles II. The figure was originally intended as a statue of the French 'Sun King', Louis XIV. The statue was being transported by sea so that the sculptor could complete the head from life, but Holmes captured the ship carrying it, took the statue and had his own likeness attached

Insight

OLD MONEY

According to local history, Yarmouth man and hero Robert Holmes (1622–92) sailed with the King's fleet to Guinea off the west coast of Africa. During this service Holmes' ship took aggressive action against a vessel that belonged to the Dutch West India Company which resulted in a large amount of Dutch gold allegedly being shipped back to England by Holmes. This gold was then melted down and made into coins – known as 'guineas'.

to it instead. Holmes entertained Charles II at his house on the quay in Yarmouth, now the George Hotel.

West of Yarmouth is Fort Victoria Country Park, based around the remains of a fort built in 1855. The many parts of the park afford superb views of the Solent, and there are guided walks, an interesting maritime heritage exhibition, a marine aquarium and planetarium – the perfect outing for all ages.

ISLE OF WIGHT

TOURIST INFORMATION CENTRES

Cowes
The Arcade, Fountain Quay.
Tel: 01983 813818

Newport
The Guildhall, High Street.
Tel: 01983 813818

Ryde
Western Esplanade. Tel: 01983 813818

Sandown
8 High Street. Tel: 01983 813818

Shanklin
67 High Street. Tel: 01983 813818

Yarmouth
The Quay. Tel: 01983 813818

PLACES OF INTEREST

Adgestone Vineyard
Brading.Tel: 01983 402503;
www.adgestonevineyard.co.uk

Appuldurcombe House
Godshill. Tel: 01983 852484;
www.english-heritage.org.uk

Barton Manor Gardens & Vineyard
East Cowes. Tel: 01983 292835

Bembridge Windmill (NT)
High Street, Bembridge.
Tel: 01983 873945;

Brading Roman Villa
Brading.
Tel: 01983 406223;
www.bradingromanvilla.org.uk

Calbourne Water Mill
Tel: 01983 531227;
www.calbournewatermill.co.uk

Carisbrooke Castle & Isle of Wight Museum (EH)
1.5 miles (2km) southeast of Newport.
Tel: 01983 522107

Fort Victoria Country Park
Near Yarmouth.
Tel: 01983 823893;
www.fortvictoria.co.uk

Heritage Museum
11 Spring Hill, Ventnor.
Tel: 01983 855407;
www.ventnorheritage.org.uk

Isle of Wight Steam Railway
Tel: 01983 884343;
www.iwsteamrailway.co.uk

Maritime Museum
Beckford Road, Cowes.
Tel: 01983 823433

Morton Manor
Brading.
Tel: 01983 406168

Mottistone Manor Garden (NT)
Tel: 01983 741302
Museum of Island History
Guildhall, Newport.
Tel: 01983 823366;
www.iwight.com
The Needles Old Battery (NT)
West Highdown, Totland.
Tel: 01983 754772
The Needles Park
Tel: 0870 458 0022;
www.theneedles.co.uk
Newport Roman Villa
Cypress Road, Newport.
Tel: 01983 529720;
www.romans-in-britain.org.uk
Nostalgia Toy Museum
High Street, Godshill.
Tel: 01983 840181
Osborne House and Gardens (EH)
East Cowes. Tel: 01983 200022
Rosemary Vineyard
Ashey, Ryde.
Tel: 01983 811084;
www.rosemaryvineyard.co.uk
Shanklin Chine
Shanklin.Tel: 01983 866432;
www.shanklinchine.co.uk

Smuggling Museum
Botanic Garden, Ventnor.
Tel: 01983 853677
Yarmouth Castle (EH)
Yarmouth.
Tel: 01983 760678

FOR CHILDREN
Amazon World Zoo Park
Watery Lane, near Arreton.
Tel: 01983 867122;
www.amazonworld.co.uk
Blackgang Chine
Chale, near Ventnor.
Tel: 01983 730052;
www.blackgangchine.com
Godshill Model Village
Old Vicarage Gardens, Godshill.
Tel: 01983 840270;
www.modelvillagegodshill.co.uk
Isle of Wight Owl and Falconry Centre
Appledurcombe.
Tel: 01983 852484;
www.appledurcombe.co.uk
Isle of Wight Zoo
Yaverland Seafront, Sandown.
Tel: 01983 403883;
www.isleofwightzoo.com

Seaview Wildlife Encounter
Tel: 01983 612261;
www.flamingoparkiw.com

SHOPPING
Arreton Barns Craft Village
Main Road, Arreton.
Tel: 01983 539361;
www.arretonbarns.co.uk
Bonchurch Pottery
Shore Road, Bonchurch.
Tel: 01983 854445
The Cider Barn
High Street, Godshill.
Tel: 01983 840680
Isle of Wight Farmers' Market
St Thomas' Square, Newport,
every Fri.

PERFORMING ARTS
Medina Theatre
Fairlee Road, Newport.
Tel: 01983 527020
Ryde Theatre
Lind Street, Ryde. Tel: 01983 568 099
Shanklin Theatre
Prospect Road, Shanklin.
Tel: 01983 862739

SPORTS & ACTIVITIES
ADRENALINE SPORTS
Wight Water Adventure Watersports
Tel: 01983 404987;
www.wightwaters.com
High Adventure
Yarmouth.
Tel: 07774 614883;
www.islandactivities.co.uk
Paragliding and fast boats.
BOAT TRIPS
Needles Pleasure Cruises
Tel: 01983 761567
CYCLE HIRE
Battersby Cycles
Ryde.
Tel: 01983 562039
Extreme Cycles
Ventnor.
Tel: 01983 852232
Wight Offroad
Tel: 01983 730120;
www.wightoffroad.co.uk
FISHING
Island Fish Farm and Meadow Lakes
Muggleton Lane, near Brighstone.
Tel: 01983 740941

Scotties Fishing Tackle
11 Lugley Street, Newport.
Tel: 01983 522115;
www.scotties-tackle.co.uk

HORSE-RIDING

Allendale Equestrian Centre
Newport Road, Godshill.
Tel: 01983 840258

Brickfields Horse Country
Binstead, near Ryde.
Tel: 01983 566801; www.brickfields.net

ANNUAL EVENTS & CUSTOMS

Cowes
Cowes Week; late Jul–early Aug.
Tel: 01983 295744;
www.cowesweek.co.uk

Newchurch
Garlic Festival, mid-Aug.
Tel: 01983 863566;
www.garlic-festival.co.uk

Newport
Isle of Wight Festival; pop festival,
mid-Jun.
Tel: 08705 321321;
www.isleofwightfestival.org

Ryde
Carnival, end Aug/early Sep.

Yarmouth
Old Gaffers Festival, gaff-rigged yachts,
early Jun.
Tel: 01983 760541;
www.yarmoutholdgaffersfestival.co.uk

Isle of Wight
Isle of Wight County Show, mid-Aug.
Northwood Showground.
Tel: 01980 813800;
www.riwas.org.uk
Isle of Wight Cycling Festival, mid-Sep.
Tel: 01983 823355;
www.sunseaandcycling.com
Isle of Wight Walking Festival, mid-May.
Tel: 01983 203888;
www.isleofwightwalkingfestival.co.uk
Round the Island Race, early Jun.
Tel: 01983 296911;
www.roundtheisland.org.uk
White Air, end Oct.
Extreme sports festival.
www.whiteair.co.uk

Vineyard Café
Adgestone Vineyard, Upper Adgestone
Road, Brading, PO36 0ES
Tel: 01983 402503
www.adgestonevineyard.co.uk
The oldest vineyard in Britain serves
some of the best cream teas on the Isle
of Wight, with freshly baked scones,
and home-made cakes. Morning coffee
and light lunches – including wine
– are also available, and check ahead
for special musical evenings.

God's Providence House
12 St Thomas Square, Newport
Tel: 01983 522085
This is the spot where, it is claimed,
the Great Plague of the 1560s came
to a halt – hence the name. Today it's
a traditional tea room, serving coffee,
teas and lunches.

Pearly Boise Ice Cream Parlour
57 High Street, Shanklin
Tel: 01983 864611
This wonderful emporium offers
home-made ice cream in 27 flavours,
including apple crumble, white
chocolate and orange Cointreau.
There are also sorbets to whet your
appetite, and traditional milkshakes
and sundaes. And for a retro treat,
enjoy a knickerbocker glory! Coffee and
pastries are also available.

The Old World Tearooms & Gardens
The High Street, Godshill
Tel: 01983 840637
This popular, family-run tea room
in the highly photogenic village of
Godshill serves delicious cream
teas, as well as morning coffee, tasty
light lunches, and a good range of
sandwiches and baguettes. Eat indoors
or outside in warmer weather.

DAY DAWN

BEMBRIDGE HOUSEBOAT

Buddle Inn
St Catherines Road, Niton
Tel: 01983 730243

This is one of the island's oldest hostelries in a former 16th-century farmhouse. There are stone flags, oak beams and a large open fire inside and dogs and muddy boots are welcome. Home-cooked food includes local crab and lobster, curries, pies and ploughman's, and there's a good choice of wines and real ales.

The Folly
Folly Lane, Cowes
Tel: 01983 297171

Easy access by both land and water makes this unusual Cowes pub a very popular venue in summer. It was constructed in part from the timbers out of the hull of an old barge, and makes good use of its nautical theme, offering a blackboard menu that includes spicy sausage 'Crewpot' casserole, or maybe fresh fish.

The New Inn
Mill Lane, Shalfleet
Tel: 01983 531314

Beamed ceilings, a flagstone floor and big open fireplaces characterise this fine 18th-century inn on the coastal path route. They specialise in fish and seafood, with unusual offerings such as Cajun-style salmon, and hake with tarragon and lemon, alongside favourites such as duck in orange sauce. There are around 60 wines, plus beers such as Flowers Bitter and Marston's Pedigree.

The Red Lion
Church Place, Freshwater
Tel: 01983 754925

The pub has a very pleasant setting on the River Yar. Everything here is freshly made. Favourites might include gammon with parsley sauce, smoked haddock pâté, and apple pie and custard. The garden includes a peaceful herb garden – the perfect place to sup a pint of local Goddards ale – and dogs are permitted.

BOTLEY

Portsmouth &
Southeast Coast

INTRODUCTION

The great Hampshire ports,
commercial Southampton and
naval-fleet based Portsmouth,
comprise the largest urban
area on England's south
coast. During the 20th century
they spread, eating up lesser
harbours and towns and
creeping inland. Among all
this urban sprawl are the
nature reserves at Langstone
Harbour and Titchfield Haven,
the popular beaches around
Southsea, and the many
marinas that line the Solent's
shores. Wartime memories
abound in this area, too
– thousands of men, women
and boats congregated here
for the invasion of occupied
Europe during World War II.

Unmissable attractions

Go to the top of Portsmouth's striking Spinnaker Tower for superb views over the British Navy's most important historical base...see the coastal differences by walking part of the Solent Way...spend, spend, spend at Southampton's glossy West Quay shopping centre...witness boat-building at its best on The Hamble...marvel at 3rd-century Roman Portchester Castle...come face to face with a shark at Southsea's fantastic Blue Reef Aquarium...visit writer William Cobbett's beloved Botley.

1 HMS *Victory*
The prow of Admiral Horatio Nelson's flagship HMS *Victory*, has been restored and can be admired at Portsmouth Maritime Museum.

2 Netley Abbey
Monastic life flourished at the abbey until the Dissolution. The structure was destroyed when it was converted into a home.

3 Spinnaker Tower
Most people choose to use the lift, rather than Climb the 572 steps to the third-view deck. Apart from the awesome panorama, there is a challenging view down through a glass floor. Do you dare to step onto it?

BOTLEY

The political writer and champion of the underdog William Cobbett farmed here between 1804 and 1817. He described this attractive redbrick village, where he was actually constantly quarrelling with the local parson, as 'the most delightful village in the world', and he is fondly celebrated with a memorable stone in the village square and a walking trail around the village. Botley remains delightful, its wide main street and busy square are dominated by a little porticoed Market Hall of 1848. The mill on the River Hamble, listed in the Domesday Book, is now a crafts centre. Botley was once a small port at the head of the Hamble River.

Just to the south is the extensive Manor Farm Country Park with 400 acres (162ha) of varied habitats, supports a range of plants and animals, with riverside and woodland walks. The park's Manor Farm Museum is a traditional farm offering hands-on experience of pigs, cows and other livestock. East of Botley, Wickham Vineyard offers a taste of English wines.

FAREHAM

Fareham's attractive old High Street has a complementary mix of architecture – 18th-century brick, Victorian stucco and earlier timber. Since World War II the old town has expanded and now merges with neighbouring parishes in a sprawl of houses and industry. Nevertheless the centre remains appealing, and visitors can appreciate the 19th-century novelist William Thackeray's description of it as a 'dear little old Hampshire town'.

During the Middle Ages Fareham was a major port, until the channels silted up. Prosperity returned in the 18th and 19th centuries with shipbuilding for the navy, and the big, attractive houses on the High Street were built for senior naval men. Today there are high-tech industries as well as an entertainment centre and a shopping

mall. Fareham Creek, popular with the yachting fraternity, is now a conservation area.

In 1784 at Funtley, near Fareham, Henry Cort invented a process of creating wrought iron which helped keep Britain's economy strong during the Napoleonic Wars. British iron ores are generally low grade, and during the wars, foreign ores could not get through – a potentially disastrous state of affairs affecting the production of horseshoes, tools and nails. Cort devised the method of 'puddling', where the molten metal was stirred with iron bars – a process that separated the ore from impurities and allowed the production of wrought iron. Little remains of the works, but what there is can be seen beside the footpath off the Wickham to Titchfield road beside the M27.

HAMBLE

Once a main site of a flourishing naval dockyard, the village of Hamble and the estuary of the little river that shares its name are still popular with sailors of the small pleasure craft that crowd its busy waters as they sail or motor in and out of Southampton Water. The older parts of the village go down to the quayside near the jetties, the marina and the boat-building yards.

Hamble was a favoured place of embarkation during the Napoleonic Wars and troops were mustered

Insight

SAILING ON THE SOLENT

The Solent is said to contain the largest pleasure sailing fleet in the world, with more than 32,000 yacht berths in the plethora of marinas along the coast stretching from Southampton Water to Chichester Harbour. The sailing is safe here, in the sheltered lagoons of Portsmouth, Langstone and Chichester harbours, in Southampton Water and in the Solent, where craft are protected from the open Channel by the Isle of Wight. Hamble is the yachting capital of Southampton Water and Ocean Village, in Southampton's old Alexandra Dock, is a superb marina where hundreds of yachts are moored, and there are plenty of shops and restaurants.

here, notably in 1794 when Lord Moira's troops assembled before crossing to Ostend. In more recent times Hamble has had strong links with the aircraft industry, with a British Aerospace factory and airfield where airline pilots are put through their paces. Near by, the village of Bursledon has the last steam-driven brickworks in the country, founded in 1897, and Hampshire's only working windmill.

HAYLING ISLAND

This small, popular island separates the tidal creeks, sprawling mudflats and low-lying saltmarshes of Langstone and Chichester harbours. The northern part is chiefly rural while the southern part, facing over the Channel, has been a resort since the mid-19th century. It has a 5-mile (8km) long sandy beach, select golf club and all the paraphernalia of a holiday resort devoted to water sports, particularly windsurfing. Drivers should note that there is only one road to and from the island, and it can get very busy.

The seafront is dominated by the huge Norfolk Crescent, erected in the early 19th century. The 13th-century church at South Hayling stands on the island's highest point

NETLEY ABBEY

– the yew tree in the churchyard is a true Saxon, probably 1,000 years old; the Saxon font is one of only a handful of that age in Hampshire.

Sandy Point to the southeast and Langstone Harbour along to the west are designated nature reserves and both are important overwintering grounds for geese and waders. Langstone Harbour is the central of three shallow lagoons and remains a mostly wild, saltmarsh-girt, muddy place. The harbour itself covers some 5,000 acres (2,025ha) and contains a 1,370-acre (555ha) RSPB reserve, at its best in September and through the winter when it is full of migrant waders, including Brent geese, dunlin, turnstones and rare black-tailed godwits. There are frequent sightings of resident oystercatchers, redshanks, herons and shelducks.

NETLEY

Netley, a Victorian town on the shores of the Solent, was formerly important for three things – its castle, its abbey and its gigantic military hospital, the Royal Victoria, built in the aftermath of the Crimean War. This was demolished in 1966, bar the domed royal chapel, and the site is now occupied by the Royal Victoria Country Park which covers more than 100 acres (40ha) of mixed woods, marshes and beach. There is a nature trail, miniature railway and some lovely walks to be enjoyed.

The ruins of Netley Abbey stand brooding in woodland next to the Solent shore. It was founded here in 1239 as a daughter house of Beaulieu and, as little is known of day-to-day life here, we must assume a most peaceful and prayerful existence on the part of the monks, until the dissolution of the monasteries. Netley Castle, on the shore near the abbey and formerly the gatehouse, was one of Henry VIII's coastal gun stations – its tall tower is Victorian, and it has been transformed into a wonderful folly with all the panoply of Gothic device (now luxury apartments).

PORTCHESTER CASTLE

This is one of the most fascinating historical sites in Britain. The massive, 20-foot (6m) high walls of a 3rd-century Roman fort sit on a little promontory on the northern shore of Portsmouth harbour, facing directly across it and out to sea. The thick walls, 10-feet (3m) deep, enclose a large area of 9 acres (3.5ha), and make it the most complete Roman fort in northern Europe.

After the Roman withdrawal from Britain, Portchester's defences were left much as they were until 1133, when a priory was founded here by Henry I. It soon shifted inland to Southwick, but Portchester's parish church is a survivor of the monastic foundation. In 1153 the Normans took over the abandoned fort and built a keep on the northwest corner, plus a wall and moat enclosing an inner bailey. The castle was further fortified at regular intervals throughout history, and in 1415 Henry V mustered his troops on the greensward of the outer bailey and led them all through the Water Gate to embark for France and the Battle of Agincourt. Later it was used as a royal country palace, and in 1535 Henry VIII and Anne Boleyn stayed here and were 'very merry'. During the Napoleonic Wars, around 4,000 French prisoners were held within the walls.

PORTSMOUTH

Portsmouth has been Britain's foremost naval base since the late 15th century, when it had the first ever dry dock. For a great view over the city, take the lift to the top of the elegant 600-foot (170m) high Spinnaker Tower, opened in 2005.

The town's biggest attraction is the collection of historic ships that can be visited in the Naval Dockyard. HMS *Victory*, launched in 1765, was Nelson's flagship at the Battle of Trafalgar in 1805 and is probably the most famous British warship; she is the oldest commissioned warship in the world. The *Mary Rose*, pride of Henry VIII's fleet, was launched

at Portsmouth in 1511, rebuilt to carry additional guns in 1536 and then sank off Southsea in July 1545, sailing to meet the French in battle, and in full view of the King who was watching from Southsea Castle. The remains of her wreck were finally raised in 1982 and are currently housed in a specially designed and constructed building. 'Permanent conservation' is under way, and there is an exhibition of the artefacts found during salvage. HMS *Warrior*, the first 'ironclad', was launched at Blackwall in 1860, the largest, fastest and most formidable warship the world had ever seen. The Dockyard also houses the redeveloped Royal Naval Museum and 'Action Stations', a thrilling high-tech Royal Naval experience using film and interactive technology.

During World War II Portsmouth was bombed heavily, and it is unfortunate that much of the rebuilding has been particularly uninspired – one building (since demolished) was voted the ugliest in Britain by readers of a certain Sunday newspaper. This being so, hurry through to the historic dockyard and follow the Millennium Promenade (Renaissance Trail) on foot through the bustling Gunwharf Quays shopping complex to The Point. Here is the oldest and most picturesque quarter of Old Portsmouth, where surviving attractive old streets have been restored, and face out onto a little harbour. This area of intricate little roads and Georgian and Victorian

houses was known as 'Spice Island', an invocation of the exotic cargoes that arrived here. Walk on the old defences or linger by the seawall in Bath Square to watch the world and the shipping go by – this is the best of Portsmouth.

The city has more than a dozen museums, including Charles Dickens' Birthplace in Old Commercial Road, but the City Museum and Art Gallery found in Museum Road is probably the best place to start. It features 'The Story of Portsmouth' and will point you in the direction of the other remaining historic buildings around the city, including the Landport Gate of 1760, the Square Tower of 1494 and the Royal Garrison Church, where Catherine of Braganza married Charles II in 1662.

There are several good reasons to visit Gosport, just across Portsmouth Harbour, including the view back to Old Portsmouth, and to see the magnificent interior of Holy Trinity Church, which

Activity

HARBOUR TRIPS

Take a relaxing boat trip around the harbour – with an informative running commentary, they give a genuine flavour of seafaring Portsmouth: modern naval vessels, ferries and the general hustle and bustle of this most important of naval ports. If taking to the sea is not for you, catch the little ferry over to Gosport, for a view back to Old Portsmouth.

contains the organ once played by Handel. The main attraction, though, is the Royal Navy Submarine Museum, with exhibits relating to underwater warfare and submarine development, and tours of HMS *Alliance*, a submarine completed at the end of World War II. Gosport's Millennium Promenade takes in Timespace, one of the world's largest vertical sundials, erected in 2005, and Explosion!, an exciting, hands-on museum of naval firepower that will appeal to all ages.

SOUTHAMPTON

Modern Southampton has been made by its docks. Its famous double tides give prolonged high water, and although the main container docks are not accessible to the public, there's a grand view of the comings and goings of cruise ships and the pleasure craft from Town Quay and Western Esplanade. This is a sprawling, thriving, working city, with attractions that include some of the best shopping along

the south coast, the fine City Art Gallery, a string of leafy green parks, and a little Maritime Museum set in a 15th-century warehouse near the shore, which tells of the great liners built here, and the last, fateful voyage of the HMS *Titanic*. The Solent Sky Aviation Museum, which offers hands-on experience of many of the exhibits (try your hand at a supersonic jet!), was founded in honour of R J Mitchell, designer of the Spitfire fighter plane which was constructed at Southampton's Supermarine Works. A flying boat in the collection is another reminder of the port's history.

Southampton was very badly hit by bombing during World War II, and much rebuilding was done in haste and very cheaply. As a result, it is an unattractive architectural mishmash, but there are some historic gems from all periods.

The most interesting area lies south of the gleaming West Quay shopping centre, and it is worth parking there to explore on foot.

The mall has many well-known street shops, including John Lewis, Waitrose and Marks & Spencer, and leads out onto Above Bar Street, a pedestrianised shopping street set above a bulky gateway, one of several last surviving fragments of

Activity

THE SOLENT WAY
This 60-mile (96km) path runs from Milford on Sea via Southampton and Portsmouth to the wild saltings of Langstone Harbour and Emsworth. The stretch from Warsash (or Hamble) to Emsworth begins along an undeveloped stretch of Solent coast between the Hamble River and Titchfield Haven, at the mouth of the River Meon, where there is a nature reserve. Beyond Titchfield Haven it goes past the beach at Lee-on-the-Solent and the lovely curve of Stokes Bay, turning inland at Gilkicker Point for the ferry from Gosport to Old Portsmouth. From here it passes Southsea to the edge of Langstone Harbour, before curving to Emsworth.

the medieval walled city. Stroll down here, passing the Dolphin Hotel – novelist Jane Austen celebrated her 18th birthday on the first-floor ballroom here in 1793. Next door is the bombed-out Church of the Holy Rood, now dedicated to the merchant seamen of the city, and including a memorial to the 500 local crew who died aboard HMS *Titanic* when she sank in 1912. Beyond nearby St Michael's, the oldest church in the city, dating to 1070, and the only one undamaged in the war, lie Bugle Street and French Street, with the Medieval Merchant's House of 1290 and the striking timbered Tudor House Museum and Garden. Another little interesting corner to explore is Oxford Street, behind Queen's Terrace, its mellow old houses now filled with trendy restaurants, and with an Edwardian pub, the London Hotel, at one corner.

On the shore, ferries leave the island for Hythe, and Ocean Village is a modern marina from where you can take a cruise of the harbour.

SOUTHSEA

Beyond the tangle of Portsmouth's streets to the east, you emerge on to Southsea Common, faced by terraces of 19th-century stucco. The grassy common overlooking the sea escaped development during the 19th century because it was used for military training, and for this gives the town its own distinctive flavour. Southsea developed as a residential suburb of Portsmouth, but the seaside location transformed it into a holiday place from the 1860s.

There is a raucous funfair at Clarence Pier. The wide Clarence Esplanade, between the common and the sea, has the Blue Reef Aquarium, the Naval War Memorial and the Southsea Castle Museum. Near by, the D-Day Museum contains the Overlord Embroidery, a tapestry depicting the Allied invasion of Normandy in June 1944, paying homage to the Bayeux Tapestry.

Further east the pier provides boat trips and plenty of amusements, while on East Parade

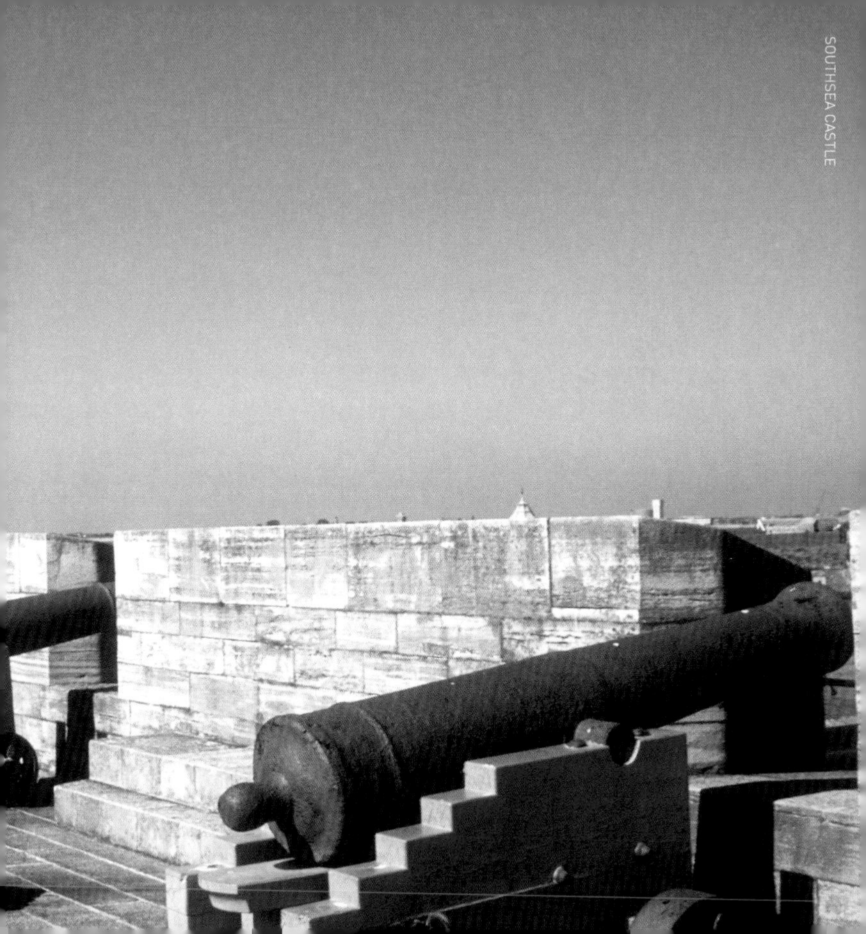

SOUTHSEA CASTLE

is the Cumberland House Natural History Museum. The Royal Marines Museum is housed in Eastney Barracks, beyond which are Port Solent and Eastney Marinas. The Solent Way goes along the sea front.

During the 1860s four sea forts were built offshore, part of the ring of forts to protect Portsmouth and Spithead from a feared attack by the French. The smallest is Spitbank Fort, which had provision for nine 38-ton guns and can be visited by ferry from Southsea pier.

TITCHFIELD

Titchfield, on the lower reaches of the River Meon, is a village of twisting roads with a charming High Street. The aerospace factories on its outskirts create a curious juxtaposition of ancient and modern. In medieval times Titchfield was a market centre and a prosperous port, with a large and thriving abbey, founded in 1232. At the Dissolution the abbey passed to Thomas Wriothesley, the 1st

Earl of Southampton, who then converted part of it into a house, but it fell into disrepair in the 18th century and is now in ruins. Little of the abbey remains but a huge Tudor gatehouse. A handsome 15th-century tithe barn stands near by. The Earl also instituted a land reclamation scheme, damming the mouth of the river and building a canal. One of England's earliest canals, it was too small for merchant ships and Titchfield's days were short-lived. The locals haven't forgiven the Earl and his effigy is burnt at celebrations in October organised by the Bonfire Boys.

A different – and magnificent – effigy of the Earl can be found in the south chapel of the church. The detailed Wriothesley Monument by artist Gerard Johnson, a Flemish refugee, was carved in 1594 and shows the 1st Earl with his wife and son. The 3rd Earl was a friend of William Shakespeare, and it is said that some of his plays received their first performance here.

TOURIST INFORMATION CENTRES

Fareham
Westbury Manor, 84 West Street.
Tel: 01329 221343

Portsmouth
Clarence Esplanade, Southsea.
Tel: 023 9282 6722

Southampton
9 Civic Centre Road. Tel: 023 8083 3333;
www.visit-southampton.co.uk

PLACES OF INTEREST

Burseldon Brickworks
Swanwick Lane, Swanwick.
Tel: 01489 576248

Bursledon Windmill
Windmill Lane, Bursledon.
Tel: 023 8040 4999;
www.hants.gov.uk/museum/windmill

Charles Dickens' Birthplace
393 Old Commercial Road,
Portsmouth.
Tel: 023 9282 7261;
www.charlesdickensbirthplace.co.uk

City Museum and Art Gallery
Museum Road, Portsmouth.
Tel: 023 9282 7261;
www.portsmouthcitymuseums.co.uk

Cumberland House Natural History Museum
Eastern Parade, Southsea.
Tel: 023 9282 7261;
www.chnhm.co.uk

D-Day Museum & Ovelord Embroidery
Clarence Esplanade, Southsea.
Tel: 023 9282 7261;
www.ddaymuseum.co.uk

Explosion! Museum of Naval Firepower
Priddy's Hard, Gosport.
Tel: 023 9250 5600;
www.explosion.org.uk

Hawthorns Urban Wildlife Centre
Southampton Common.
Tel: 023 8067 1921;
www.southampton.gov.uk/leisure

Manor Farm Country Park & Farm Museum
Pylands Lane, Bursledon.
Tel: 01489 787055;
www.hants.gov.uk/manorfarm

Maritime Museum
Town Quay, Southampton.
Tel: 023 8063 5904

Netley Abbey (English Heritage)
Tel: 023 8045 5157

Portchester Castle (English Heritage)
Castle Street, Portchester.
Tel: 0239 237 8291
Portsmouth Historic Dockyard
Victory Gate, HM Naval Base.
Tel: 023 9286 1512/9766;
www.historicdockyard.co.uk
Royal Armouries
Fort Nelson, Portsdown Hill Road,
Fareham.
Tel: 01392 233734;
www.royalarmouries.org
Royal Marines Museum
Southsea.
Tel: 023 9281 9385;
www.royalmarinesmuseum.co.uk
Royal Navy Submarine Museum
Haslar Jetty Road, Gosport.
Tel: 023 9252 9217;
www.rnsubmus.co.uk
Royal Victoria Country Park
Tel: 023 8045 5157;
www.hants.gov.uk/rvcp
Southampton City Art Gallery
Civic Centre.
Tel: 023 8083 2277;
www.southampton.gov.uk/art

Southsea Castle Museum
Clarence Esplanade.
Tel: 023 9282 7261;
www.southseacastle.co.uk
Spinnaker Tower
Gunwharf Quays, Portsmouth.
Tel: 02392 857520;
www.spinnakertower.co.uk
Titchfield Haven National Nature Reserve
Hill Head, by Stubbington.
Tel: 01329 662145;
www.hants.gov.uk/titchfield
Wickham Vineyard
Botley Road, Shedfield.
Tel: 01329 834042;
www.wickhamvineyard.co.uk

FOR CHILDREN
Blue Reef Aquarium
Clarence Esplanade, Southsea.
Tel: 023 9287 5222;
www.bluereefaquarium.co.uk
Hampshire Mega-Maze
Forty Acres Farm, Havant Road,
Havant.Tel: 023 9247 2854;
www.forty-acres.co.uk

The Pyramids Centre
Clarence Esplanade, Southsea.
Tel: 023 9279 9977;
www.pyramids.co.uk

SHOPPING
Bargate Markets
Bargate, Southampton.
Friday market, plus Farmers Markets
one Sat per month;
www.hampshirefarmersmarkets.co.uk
There are artists Markets, last Sun of
each month;
www.eatsouthampton.com
Gunwharf Quays
Portsmouth.
www.gunwharf-quays.com
The Mall Marlands Shopping Centre
Civic Centre Road, Southampton.
Tel: 023 8033 9164;
www.themall.co.uk/marlands
West Quay Shopping Centre
Tel: 023 8033 6828;
www.west-quay.co.uk
Whitely Village Outlet Shopping
Close to junction 9, M27.

PERFORMING ARTS
Kings Theatre
Albert Road, Southsea.
Tel: 023 92 828282;
www.kings-southsea.com
The Mayflower
Commercial Road, Southampton.
Tel: 023 8071 1811;
www.the-mayflower.com
New Theatre Royal
20–24 Guildhall Walk, Portsmouth.
Tel: 023 9264 9000;
www.newtheatreroyal.com
Nuffield Theatre
University Road, Southampton.
Tel: 023 8067 1771

SPORTS & ACTIVITIES
BOAT TRIPS
Blue Funnel Cruises
Ocean Village, Southampton.
Tel: 023 8022 3278;
www.bluefunnel.co.uk
Blue Star Boats
River Hamble
Tel: 023 8045 3542;
www.bluestarboats.co.uk

SS Shieldhall
47 Berth, Eastern Dock, Southampton,
Dock Gate 4.
Tel: 023 8022 5853;
www.ss-shieldhall.co.uk

HORSE-RIDING
Gleneagles Equestrian Centre
Allington Lane, West End,
Southampton.
Tel: 023 8047 3370

WALKING
The Solent Way
A 60-mile (96km) long-distance walk
from Milford on Sea to Emsworth.
Hayling Billy Trail
A 4-mile (6km) trail between Havant
and Langston.
The Strawberry Trail
15-mile (24km) circular walk in the
Hamble Valley.

ANNUAL CUSTOMS & EVENTS
Botley
Summer Festival, end Jun.
Hamble
Carnival week, early Jun.
Tel: 023 8045 7935;
www.hambleevents.org.uk

Bursledon
Swanwick, Bursledon and Warsash
Regatta
Around Elephant Boatyard, end Aug.
Tel: 023 8045 6969;
www.bursledonregatta.co.uk.

Netley
Fireworks Spectacular
Royal Victoria Country Park, around
5 Nov.
Tel: 023 8045 5157
Netley Marsh Steam & Craft Show
Meadow Mead Farm, mid-Jul.
Tel: 023 8086 7882; www.
netleymarshsteamandcraftshow.org.

Southampton
Annual Kite Festival
Lordshill, mid-Jun.
The Big Southampton Boat Show,
mid-Sep. Tel: 0870 060 0246

Titchfield
Carnival and bonfire, last Mon in Oct.

TEA ROOMS

Country Kitchens Tea Rooms
6 High Street, Botley, SO30 2EA
Tel: 01489 789161
Drop into this village tea room for cream teas in summer, plus hot and cold food and sandwiches.

The Pantry Tea Room
Manor Farm Country Park,
Pylands Lane, Bursledon, SO30 2ER
Tel: 01489 787055
In a perfect rural setting of this old farmstead, tuck into a snack, ice cream or a full-blown, home-cooked meal.

Tower Café Bar
Spinnaker Tower, Gunwharf Quays,
Portsmouth, PO1 3TT
Tel: 02392 857520
www.spinnakertower.co.uk
Take your morning coffee or afternoon tea in style (not at the top!) in Portsmouth's newest venue. Sandwiches and cakes give way to wine and beer in the evenings, as you sit and watch the sun go down.

The Village Tea Rooms
High Street, Hamble, SO31 4HA
Tel: 023 8045 5583
Just down from the main square in the village, in a 300-year old house that was once the local coffin-maker's premises, this cosy tea room doubles as a gift shop and gallery of local art and crafts, and spills out into the pretty back garden in summer. Try the Hamble Cream Special, with scones, cream and preserves, or home-made cakes and shortbread, or come early for the Skipper's Choice Breakfast.

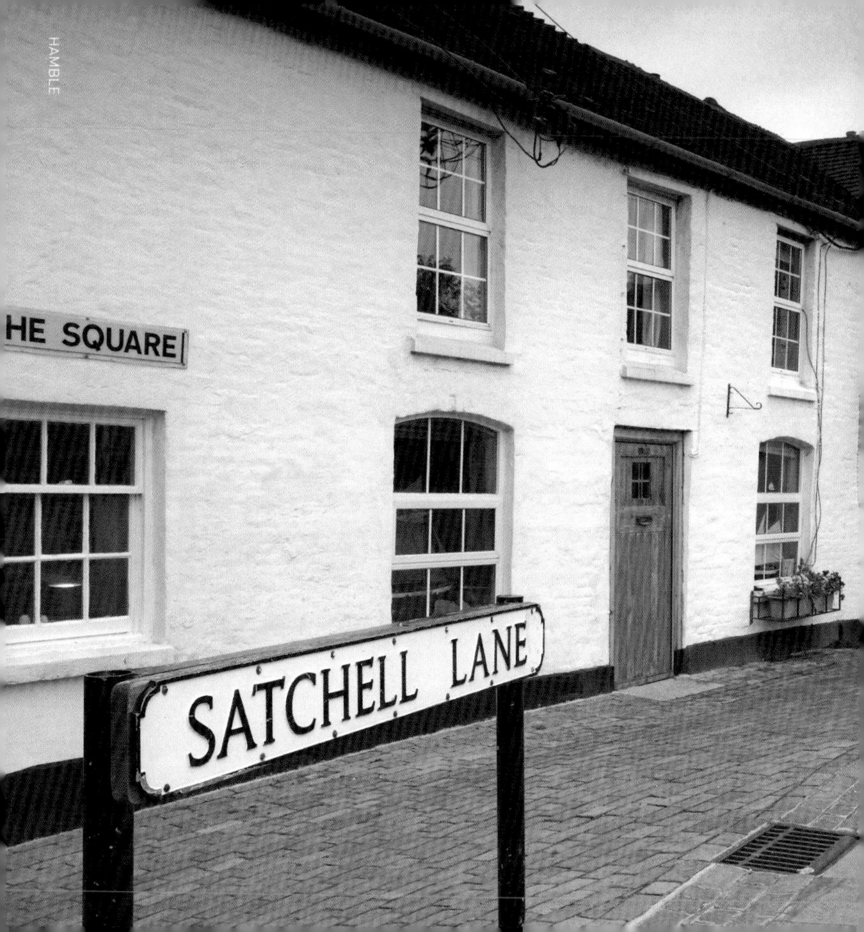
HE SQUARE
SATCHELL LANE

BURSLEDON

The Cowherds
The Common, Southampton, SO15 7NN
Tel: 023 8051 6921

On the A33, at the heart of Southampton Common, this pub was once the haunt of cattle drovers on their way to London. Now it's the perfect spot for lunch or dinner – try the ham hock with mustard sauce, or perhaps the pork, apple and cider sausages with Cheddar mash. There's a patio and inside it's cosy with open fires, oak beams and wood panelling.

Greens Restaurant & Pub
The Square, Wickham, PO17 5JQ
Tel: 01329 833197

Set on a coner of Wickham's picturesque square, and close to the River Meon, the menus at this mock-Tudor pub make good use of fresh ingredients, from smoked duck salad with pear chutney to delicious apricot-glazed bread-and-butter pudding. Food is not served on Mondays. Beers include Hopback Summer Lightning and Fullers London Pride.

The Jolly Sailor
Lands End Road, Burseldon, SO31 8DN
Tel: 023 8040 5557

This appealing old pub, overlooking Hamble marina, achieved fame in the 1980s as a location for BBC TV's salty soap opera, Howard's Way. The menus include a variety of offerings, from moules marinière and bouillabaisse to chunky sandwiches. Beers include Fursty Ferret and Tanglefoot.

The Still & West
2 Bath Square, Old Portsmouth, PO1 2JL
Tel: 023 9282 1567

At the top of Broad Street, and close to HMS Victory, this nautically themed 1504 pub has great views over the harbour and to the Isle of Wight. As you might expect, there's lots of fish on the menu, including a trademark grill of fresh fish and mussels, and delicious seafood paella.

Winchester & Salisbury

- ALRESFORD
- AMPFIELD
- AVINGTON PARK
- FARLEY MOUNT
- MOTTISFONT
- ROMSEY
- SALISBURY
- SHAFTESBURY
- STOCKBRIDGE
- WINCHESTER

INTRODUCTION

Winchester, England's ancient capital, lies amid rolling chalkland scenery, with roads radiating outwards from it across the county. To the north and west, are two contrasting landscapes: the wide chalklands of 'High Hampshire', lonely and open, dotted here and there with clumps of dark green yews and graceful beeches, and the fisherman's Hampshire – shallow green valleys of water meadows and sparkling streams that bring anglers to try their skill in England's most famous trout rivers. This is an area of unhurried little roads, great houses and gardens, tranquil rivers and sweeping views.

Unmissable attractions

Stroll in lovely Hillier Gardens, where you will witness a blaze of colour whatever the season...gain an insight into the life of Lord Mountbatten at Broadlands, a magnificent mansion...savour the haunting atmosphere of Salisbury Cathedral as you listen to the pure harmonies of its choir...test your stamina by climbing Shaftesbury's much-photographed and filmed, cobbled Gold Hill...admire the grandeur of Mottisfont Abbey...amble beside the sparkling watercress beds at Alresford...fly-fish for trout on the River Test then retreat to The Mayfly to swap stories of 'the one that got away'... visit the cathedral city of Winchester, steeped in historical fact and folklore.

3 Great Hall, Winchester
The only remaining intact part of Winchester Castle now houses the top of a painted table. Once claimed as King Arthur's famous Round Table, tests have shown that it probably dates from Tudor times.

1 Watercress Line
The great days of steam rail travel has been revived on this line which runs between Alresford and Alton. When constructed in the mid-19th century, the line ran from Winchester to Alton. The track and trains are maintained by a team of enthusiastic volunteers.

2 Hillier Gardens
Sir Harold Hillier established this arboretum in 1953 in the grounds of his home. The superb plant collection extends over 180 acres (72ha).

4 Old Sarum

William the Conqueror built a castle in Old Sarum soon after his arrival in England. Eventually a cathedral was built in the grounds but in the 13th century this was moved to nearby Salisbury; the castle eventually went into decline.

5 Salisbury Cathedral

Building work on the cathedral began in 1220; an army of dedicated labourers and craftsmen toiled for around 40 years to complete the cathedral. The magnificent tower and famous spire were added in the 14th century.

4

ALRESFORD

Lovely Alresford, with its wide streets of friendly Georgian houses of brick and stucco, lies in the broad valley of the River Alre, hence the name (pronounced 'Allsford'). It is really two places – Old Alresford to the north of the river, which is now no more than a village with an adjoining park, and New Alresford, the busy market town to the south which was 'New' in about 1200. Between the two is Alresford Pond, created by Bishop de Lucy in the 13th century. Its dam, the Great Weir, is the largest non-military medieval earthwork in England and the only one that still serves this original dual purpose of dam and road causeway. Today its 30 acres (12ha) are a haven for wildlife and also feed the famous local watercress beds.

New Alresford retains its medieval street plan, with a T-shape formed by the spacious elegant Broad Street and West and East Streets, the old Winchester–London road. A borough by 1294, New Alresford soon became one of England's ten greatest wool markets. Two of its mills survive, the Town Mill and the old Fulling Mill. Fires devastated New Alresford between the early 15th century and 1689, which accounts for its mainly Georgian appearance.

Approach from Old Alresford or from Bishop's Sutton for the most attractive introduction to the town – the south approach from Cheriton leads through less inviting modern suburbs. Strolling through New Alresford is a delight. The town has a variety of interesting shops, chic boutiques and some excellent craft workshops, and Broad Street, with its line of lime trees and pretty old fashioned lamps, is one of Hampshire's finest streets.

Mary Russell Mitford, author of the classic Our Village, was born at 27 Broad Street in 1787 and lived there until she was ten, when she moved with her father to Three Mile Cross near Reading – the village of her book. She later wrote, 'Alresford

LAURENCE

is or will be celebrated in history for two things: the first, to speak modestly, is my birth, the second is cricket'. Few today would associate Alresford with cricket, but Taylor of Alresford, a member of the famous Hambledon Club was born here, and cricket writer and commentator John Arlott once lived at the Old Sun. Today Alresford is better known for its watercress beds and its steam railway, the Watercress Line.

North of Alresford, Northington Grange is the dramatic empty shell of a neoclassical mansion, where the 1999 movie *Onegin* was filmed.

AMPFIELD

In rolling countryside to the southwest of Winchester, this little village, set among beech woods and vast cornfields, is best known for the nearby Hillier Gardens. Sir Harold Hillier, the great plantsman, began his famous collection of trees and shrubs on the Ampfield estate in 1953. It became one of the largest in the world, with some 40,000 temperate plants originating from every continent. There is colour at every season of the year with witch hazels, rhododendrons, autumn foliage and herbaceous perennials.

The heart of the village is at Knapp, now designated a conservation area. There were clay pits and a pottery near by, and the well-known Potters Heron Hotel preserves in its name a shadowy recollection of the old industry, since a potter's treadle wheel is also known as a 'hern' or 'heron'. In much later times this same clay was used to make the bricks for the Church of St Mark, built between 1838 and 1841 at the instigation of John Keble, a famous member of the High Church Oxford Movement, who was vicar at nearby Hursley.

Ampfield has literary associations. Richard Morley, the 17th-century 'Hedge Poet', lived here and the Rev W Awdry, author of the *Thomas the Tank Engine* books, spent his boyhood in Ampfield, where his father was the vicar.

AVINGTON PARK

Avington Park lies between Easton and Alresford, east of Winchester. Dating mainly to the early 18th century, but with some parts much earlier, it is a big rose-pink house with a splendid portico and

ROYAL ASSIGNATIONS

Avington Park's owner, George Brydges, had as his patron no less a personage than Charles II. The King and his mistress, Nell Gwynn, would stay at Avington during the six weeks of Winchester's horse-racing season. More royal assignations were reputed to have taken place here about 150 years later, when George IV would enjoy private meetings here with his mistress, Mrs Fitzherbert.

some wonderful interior features, including a painted ceiling by Verrio and a fine colonnade in the 19th-century conservatory. In November 1825 William Cobbett rode through on his way from Easton, and described the scene: '...The house is close down at the edge of the meadow land; there is a lawn before it, and a pond supplied by the Itchen...We looked down on all this from a rising ground, and the water, like a looking-glass, showed

us the trees, and even the animals. This certainly is one of the prettiest spots in the world...' The views to the house across the lake and parkland seem little changed.

The brick-built Church of St Mary was built in from 1768 to 1771 by Margaret, Marchioness of Carnarvon. It preserves the air of the 18th century as verily as the view over the park.

A large monument to the Marchioness, who died in 1768, is in pink and white marble with two urns and an obelisk. Another monument is to John Shelley, brother of the famous poet, who purchased Avington Park in 1847.

FARLEY MOUNT

Farley Mount Country Park covers over 1,000 acres (405ha) of chalk upland west of Winchester and east of the broad Test valley. At 586 feet (178m), it remains the highest point in the region and there are wonderful views in all directions. Its most prominent feature is the

pyramid folly, a memorial raised in 1734 to a horse who bravely won its race despite having fallen the previous day into a chalk pit while out hunting. The horse was renamed Beware Chalk Pit.

This popular country park is best known for its variety of habitats, with short turf, mixed woodland and Forestry Commission plantation. There is plenty of wildlife in the old oak, beech and yew woods and also in the great swathes of ancient coppicing. Orchids are plentiful and there are a number of nature trails in Crab Wood, on the east side of the park. Car parks are clearly marked. The park is crossed by the Roman road from the Mendip silver-lead mines and Old Sarum to Winchester, and by the Clarendon Way long-distance footpath.

MOTTISFONT

The little village of Mottisfont lies in that part of the wide green Test valley where the trees seem to be exceptionally large, the streams of the river are particularly numerous and the atmosphere breathes peace and prosperity. The village's name is derived from the spring or 'font' which rises where the village 'moot' was held in Saxon times.

A house of Augustinian canons was founded here in 1201, which at the Dissolution passed to Lord Sandys, in exchange for the then villages of Paddington and Chelsea. Unusually, it was the church that he converted into his mansion, demolishing the residential parts of the priory. The Tudor building was remodelled in the 18th century by the Mills family, to whom it had passed, giving rise to the present mellow house.

Today Mottisfont Abbey is famed for its drawing room, decorated in Gothic trompe l'oeil style by Rex Whistler in 1938, and for Derek Hill's 20th-century picture collection. The tranquil grounds have sweeping lawns which run down to the River Test, and the walled garden houses the superb National Collection of old roses, at their best in June.

ROMSEY

This small town on the River Test is dominated by its magnificent Abbey Church of 1120–70, a handsome Norman building with a low, square tower, massive walls, a splendid south doorway and an interior of beautifully carved Norman arches. It contains two remarkable Saxon stone carvings from earlier churches

ROMSEY ABBEY

on the site, and its treasures include the *Romsey Psalter* (a 15th-century illuminated manuscript), and a monument to the noted economist Sir William Petty (1623–87), born in Romsey and a founder member of the Royal Society. Lord Mountbatten of Burma (1900–79), one-time confidant to Prince Charles, is buried in the abbey.

Romsey is an attractive place with many pleasing streets of Georgian and later houses. It centres on spacious Market Place, which has a statue in the middle of Lord Palmerston, the Victorian statesman who lived at Broadlands. The 13th-century timbered King John's House, opposite the Abbey Church, is said to be where John's daughter lived before she married the Scottish king. There is a lovely park with a bandstand, beside the River Test.

Across the river are the gates of Broadlands, a Palladian mansion with a great 18th-century portico, set in a landscaped park that was created by 'Capability' Brown. Once the home of Lord Palmerston, more

Visit

ROMSEY ABBEY

The nuns of Romsey Abbey were almost wiped out by the Black Death, and after the Dissolution the church was purchased by the people of Romsey who, until then, had worshipped under sufferance in the north transept. We must be grateful to those Tudor townsfolk who raised the necessary £100 to buy the church, since not only Hampshire but all England would be the poorer without this wonderful parish church, the largest in the county.

recently of Lord Mountbatten and now of Lord Romsey, it houses exhibitions on Mountbatten's life and a spectacular Mountbatten audio-visual presentation in the stable block. The house contains many fine works of art including several pieces by Van Dycks. Rooms include the stately Saloon and a powder-blue Wedgwood Room. Furniture by Ince and Mayhew was made specifically for the house.

To the east, the churchyard of East Wellow contains the grave of Florence Nightingale (1820–1920), the founder of modern nursing. The church has some unusual 13th-century wall paintings.

SALISBURY

Old Sarum's history dates back to a time long before records were made, but the giant earthwork is founded on an Iron Age camp that covered 56 acres (22ha). The earliest settlers were followed by Romans, Anglo-Saxons, Danes and Normans – William the Conqueror reviewed his troops here in 1070.

A Norman castle and cathedral were erected, but water was scarce on this plain, and the military and ecclesiastical factions could not agree who should take precedence. Accordingly, in 1220 a new cathedral was planned to the south in nearby New Sarum – or Salisbury – using stones from the old one. It seems that the spirit went out of Old Sarum in more ways than one, as the castle fell into decay, and the town was gradually abandoned. There's not much to see of this once-thriving settlement today, but for the excavated foundations of the old cathedral and fragments of the castle, but the earthwork itself is fairly impressive and the panoramic views make the walk worthwhile..

And so, while Winchester's old heart may seem a bit like a medieval muddle, Salisbury feels comparatively spacious and regular – it was planned and built on a grid, beside the River Avon. Many streets are named after the goods that were sold there – Fish Row, Butchers Row, and so on. Some have been pedestrianised, and highlights to look out for include the 16th-century façade of the Joiner's Hall on St Ann Street and the 18th-century Guildhall. The Poultry Cross in Silver Street dates to the 15th century.

Unusually, the Gothic cathedral was built in almost one go, the majority of it being completed by 1258, at a cost of around £27,000.

The main exception is its soaring spire, 404ft (123m) high, which was added in the 14th century and is the structure's most identifiable feature, painted most memorably by John Constable from across the water meadows in 1823. A climb up 332 steps and through the cathedral's roof spaces takes you to the top of the tower for far-reaching views over the city and around.

Salisbury cathedral's interior was unfortunately drastically remodelled in the 18th century by James Wyatt, who 'decluttered' the interior by clearing screens and tombs and throwing out some of the old stained glass. Wyatt also covered over the 13th-century roof painting in the choir, but this was later restored. Today one of the most striking features is the intense blue 'Prisoners of Conscience Window' in the Trinity Chapel.

Two of the cathedral's most prized possessions are the clock of 1386, the oldest in England, and an original copy of the Magna

Visit

CATHEDRAL CHOIR

There has been a choir at Salisbury Cathedral for around 800 years, and today it is famous for admitting girls as well as boys. Children as young as seven years old can join the choir school, though they face tough competition to get into the school, taking part in regular lessons alongside their daily two singing practices. Hear them during term time at evensong and at special services throughout the year.

Insight

ST ANN'S GATE

Above St Ann's ancient gateway, built in the 14th century, into the inner city of Salisbury is a small chapel, which became the music room for Malmesbury House. It is said that the great composer Frederick Handel (1685–1759) gave his first public performance in England in this chamber in 1710. The royal coat of arms on the gateway refers to a visit by Charles II in 1665, when he stayed here to avoid an outbreak of plague in London.

SALISBURY CATHEDRAL

Carta, the 'great document' forced by rebellious barons on King John at Runnymede in 1215, to limit the monarch's more arbitrary powers. It's surprisingly small for such a significant document, about A3 size.

A stroll around the extensive cathedral close is essential, including gracious old houses such as the Old Deanery, and the King's House, now home to the Salisbury and South Wiltshire Museum, which includes finds from Stonehenge, watercolours by Turner, history relating to Old Sarum, and the Warminster Jewel. Mompesson House is a gem in Queen Anne style, with notable plasterwork and a pretty walled garden, and played a starring role in the 1995 film of Jane Austen's *Sense and Sensibility*. The Wardrobe contains an interesting military museum.

The 17th-century Palladian mansion of Wilton House, home of the Earl of Pembroke, lies west of the town, and is well worth a look for its famous Single and Double Cube

Visit

OLD WARDOUR

Northeast of the town, just off the A30 to Salisbury, lies Old Wardour Castle, a romantic ruin in a beautiful landscaped setting. The castle had a unique formation, with a pair of square towers sitting at the entrance and an elegant hexagonal shaped courtyard in the middle. It was started in 1392 as a grand mansion rather than for defence, but was twice besieged during the Civil War, first by Parliamentarians and later by Royalists, and both armies caused such damage that the castle was abandoned. In 1769 New Wardour Castle, a Palladian mansion, was built about 1 mile (1.6km) away.

Rooms and its elegant gardens. The house was also the most unlikely setting for the D-Day landings headquarters during World War II; more recently, scenes from *Sense and Sensibility*, *The Madness of King George*, *Mrs Brown* and *Pride and Prejudice* were filmed here.

SHAFTESBURY

The idyllic view from the top of Gold Hill in Shaftesbury, with the line of cottages tipping down the steep cobbled road ahead and a perfect panorama to of rolling green Dorset hills behind, is one of the best known in England. You are bound to have seen it before – it is used as the backdrop of many a TV period costume drama, and most famously at the centre of the 1970s Hovis bread television adverts, revived in 2006. In fact, thanks in part to the publicity generated by the original Hovis ads, the cobbled road and 700-year-old buttressed abbey walls opposite were given a much needed restoration and make-over in 1980. Today it is a totally pedestrian zone and genuinely charming despite all the hype, though your knees may complain of the steepness after a walk down and back.

The abbey was founded in AD 888, on the edge of Cranborne Chase, by King Alfred for his daughter Aethelgifu and a community of Benedictine nuns. Edward the Martyr, murdered at Corfe Castle, was buried here in 979, making it a very popular (as well as prosperous) site of pilgrimage, and the Danish King Canute insisted that his heart should be interred in the abbey after his death in 1035. In 1539 it was abandoned as part of the dissolution of monasteries that took place across England, and today you can stroll around the low ruins, admire the remains of the Abbey Church, and learn more at the associated museum with its large Anglo Saxon herb garden.

Shaftesbury Town Museum stands at the top of Gold Hill, and celebrates this historic market town which grew fat on the profits of cereals and dairy produce from Cranborne Chase and the near by Blackmore Vale (and the town still fills up for Thursday markets). Traditional Dorsetshire bonnets and button-making were two of the small-scale industries of the town in years gone by.

Just off Bell Street, Swan's Yard is home to many local craftspeople and artists, and is well worth exploring. Another favourite corner is the Pump Yard, near the Olde Two Brewers Inn. It's a delightful little private courtyard of restored houses facing onto St James Street, with an old pump at the centre.

STOCKBRIDGE

Lying deep in the broad Test valley, and spanning that many-streamed river on an artificial causeway constructed in Roman times, Stockbridge consists of a gracious wide street lined with an attractive variety of little houses and shops, with open views eastwards to the hills. It feels as if it should be the main thoroughfare of a sizeable town, but it is not, and behind the elegant façades, the gift and antiques shops, the art galleries and the hotels are the water meadows of the River Test. Some of the river's streamlets, teeming with trout, flow under and alongside the main street.

The most prestigious of English angling clubs, The Houghton, has its headquarters at the suitably fitting Grosvenor Hotel, Stockbridge's most impressive building, with a great pillared porch that juts out into the street and a room above. The town was on a main drovers' route between Wales and Surrey and Kent, and sheep fairs were regularly held here from Tudor times until the early 20th century.

Stockbridge Common Marsh is ancient land in the care of the National Trust, as is the open Stockbridge Down, where there is a large Bronze Age cemetery consisting of 15 round barrows.

Northwest of Stockbridge, on the A343, is the Museum of Army Flying at Middle Wallop airfield, which celebrates the history of army aviation. Fascinating exhibits include an Argentine Huey helicopter, captured during the Falklands War, and there are plenty hands-on games and activities designed to keep children entertained.

Insight

FISHING THE TEST

The River Test is famous throughout the world for its trout fishing, which has now become one of the most exclusive leisure pursuits in the country. Fishing above and below Stockbridge town is controlled by two famous – and expensive – clubs, which were founded in the early 19th century and now have waiting lists for its membership. The Leckford Club fishes above the village and the prestigious Houghton Club fishes the 10-mile (16km) stretch below the Leckford water.

WINCHESTER

Home to the world's longest medieval cathedral and one of Britain's great public (fee-paying) schools, and with a story that stretches back from Roman times, Winchester provides a heady walk through two millennia of history, along its main street, through alleys and gardens, past charitable almshouses and around the Cathedral Close. The city's sheer physical beauty and prized position by water meadows, has a well-heeled air that permeates the speciality and high street shops, classy eating places and Britain's largest farmers' market. The Square and Parchment Street are best for independent shops and there are many more in Little and Great Minster, St Thomas and Southgate Streets, all near to the cathedral. There's a good park-and-ride at junction 10 off the M3, and the Bikeabout scheme gives free 24-hour loan of a bike from Gladstone Street car park near the railway station and the Tourist Information Centre. Summer festivals get the city into full swing, particularly the Hat Fair in July, when some often outrageously forward street theatre takes place, and audience participation can hardly be avoided.

Although, physically, Winchester may be relatively small. Spiritually, emotionally and historically it is large indeed. It was founded shortly before the Romans came, at an important crossing point of the River Itchen. A glance at a map shows how Roman roads radiate from the city like the spokes of a wheel, and certainly Roman Winchester – Venta Belgarum – was as important as this road pattern suggests.

Winchester declined when the Romans left, so that when the shires were created in the 8th century, it did not give its name to the new county. Within a century the situation had been reversed and *Vintanceastir*, as Bede called it, was again ascendant. Alfred the Great made it capital of the West Saxons in AD 871 – Hamo Thorneycroft's statue of him stands at the foot of the High Street – and Winchester remained the capital of Wessex and, in a sense, of England, well into Norman times.

The city's prestige began to dwindle once the Treasury moved to London, but the aura of past greatness still lingers and it has been said that Winchester's fine High Street has 'a greater wealth

of historical associations than any other street in England'. Here you will find the glorious Buttercross, the Guildhall of 1713 (now a bank) with its overhanging City Clock, the arcaded, timbered row known as the Pentice, and the imposing 14th-century Westgate, a small fortified gateway that once served as a debtors' prison. Explore the little alleyways off here for a feel of the old medieval city – Abbey Passage, just below the Victorian Guildhall, is one of the best.

Winchester Castle, where both kings Henry III and Henry VIII's elder brother, Arthur, were born, was destroyed during the Civil War and only the Great Hall remains. The great round table-top which hangs on the west wall has been linked to King Arthur, but was probably made in Tudor times.

The mighty cathedral does not dominate the city, but sits long and low among the trees and lawns of its lovely close. The present solid, squat Norman building was

begun in 1097 by Bishop Wakelin on a floating foundation of logs, for the site was half swamp. In the 14th century Bishop William of Wykeham transformed it into what we see today, replacing the flat roof with great ribs and detailed mouldings, adding tall clustered columns around the original piers, and he introduced vast, spacious, elegant fan vaulting. The cathedral is dedicated to St Swithun (died AD 862), who was bishop here, and his tomb lies in the cathedral. Also here is the tomb of William II (Rufus) and a plain slab to the novelist, Jane Austen, who died near by in College Street in 1817. Look out for delights such as the richly patterned medieval floor tiles, and a stained-glass window in memory of Izaak Walton, the famous angler. During school term time, evensong is sung by the cathedral choir at 5.30pm, Monday to Saturday, and 3.30pm Sunday. Parts of the cathedral doubled as the Vatican for the very popular 2006 movie, *The Da Vinci Code*.

The cathedral close contains part of the priory destroyed by Henry VIII's officers, and the City Museum, while near by lie the ruins of the enormous Bishops' Palace, Wolvesey, largely demolished in 1800. The buildings of Winchester College, England's oldest public school, founded in 1387, lie at the end of College Street, and may be toured. A mile (1.6km) to the south, and overlooking the River Itchen, you'll find the Hospital of St Cross – fine almshouses that date from the 12th century, with a Norman church and an ancient tradition of providing beer and bread for wayfarers, still given today on request.

South of Winchester, Marwell Zoo is set in rolling parkland and has a worldwide selection including lemurs, tropical creepy-crawlies, zebras, tigers, white rhinos and meerkats. Free road trains make getting around the vast 100-acre (40.5ha) park easy, and there are animal shows and 'meet the keeper' sessions in summer.

TOURIST INFORMATION CENTRES

Romsey
Heritage and Visitor Centre, Church
Street. Tel: 01794 512987

Salisbury
Fish Row. Tel: 01722 334956;
www.visitsalisbury.com

Shaftesbury
8 Bell Street. Tel: 01747 853514;
www.ruraldorset.co.uk

Winchester
The Guildhall, High Street.
Tel: 01962 840500;
www.visitwinchester.co.uk

PLACES OF INTEREST

Avington Park
Winchester.
Tel: 01962 779260;
www.avingtonpark.co.uk

Broadlands
Romsey.
Tel: 01794 505010; www.broadlands.net

Farley Mount Country Park
West of Winchester.
Tel: 01962 860984;
www.hants.gov.uk/countryside

The Grange (English Heritage)
Northington, near Alresford.
Tel: 02392 581059

Sir Harold Hillier Gardens
Jermyns Lane, Ampfield, by Romsey.
Tel: 01794 369318;
www.hilliergardens.org.uk

Hospital of St Cross
St Cross Road, Winchester.
Tel: 01962 851375;
www.stcrosshospital.co.uk

King John's House & Tudor Cottage
Church Street, Romsey.
Tel: 01794 512200;
www.romseyheritage.org.uk

Mompesson House (National Trust)
Cathedral Close, Salisbury.
Tel: 01722 335659

Mottisfont Abbey Garden (National Trust)
Near Romsey. Tel: 01794 340575

Museum of Army Flying
Middle Wallop, Stockbridge.
Tel: 01264 784421;
www.flying-museum.org.uk

Old Wardour Castle (EH)
Southwest of Tisbury, Shaftesbury.
Tel: 01747 870487

Old Sarum (English Heritage)
Castle Road, Salisbury.
Tel: 01722 335398
Redcoats Military Museum
The Wardrobe, Cathedral Close,
Salisbury.
Tel: 01722 419419;
www.thewardrobe.org.uk
Romsey Abbey
Church Place, Romsey.
Tel: 01794 513125
Salisbury & South Wiltshire Museum
The King's House,
65 The Close, Salisbury.
Tel: 01722 332151;
www.salisburymuseum.org.uk
Salisbury Cathedral
Cathedral Close.
Tel: 01722 555120;
www.salisburycathedral.org.uk
Shaftesbury Abbey Museum & Garden
Park Walk, Shaftesbury.
Tel: 01747 852910;
www.shaftesburyabbey.fsnet.co.uk
Shaftesbury Town Museum & Garden
Gold Hill.
Tel: 01747 852157

The Watercress Line
The Railway Station, Station Road,
Alresford.
Tel: 01962 734866;
www.watercressline.co.uk
Wilton House
Wilton, Salisbury.
Tel: 01722 746720;
www.wiltonhouse.co.uk
Winchester Castle & Great Hall
Castle Avenue.
Tel: 01962 846476
Winchester Cathedral
The Close.
Tel: 01962 857200;
www.winchester-cathedral.org.uk
Winchester City Mill (NT)
Bridge Street, Winchester.
Tel: 01962 870057
Winchester City Museum
The Square, Winchester.
Tel: 01962 848269;
www.winchester.gov.uk
Winchester College tours
College Street, Winchester.
Tel: 01962 621209

FOR CHILDREN
Intech – the Family Science Centre
Telegraph Way, Morn Hill.
Tel: 01962 863791; www.intech-uk.com
Marwell Zoological Park
Colden Common, Winchester.
Tel: 01962 777407; www.marwell.org.uk
Family-friendly zoo.

SHOPPING
Broughton Crafts Ltd
High Street, Stockbridge.
Tel: 01264 810513
Cadogan & James
31A The Square, Winchester.
Tel: 01962 840805;
www.cadoganandcompany.co.uk
Superb delicatessen.
Fisherton Mill
108 Fisherton Street, Salisbury.
Tel: 01722 415121;
www.fishertonmill.co.uk
Contemporary art, furniture and
sculpture.
Justice
80 Parchment Street, Winchester.
Tel: 01962 850890; www.justice.co.uk
Designer jewellery.

MARKETS
Salisbury
Market, Tue and Sat; Farmers'
Markets, alternate Weds.
Shaftesbury
Market day, every Thu.

PERFORMING ARTS
Chesil Theatre
Chesil Street, Winchester.
Tel: 01962 867086;
www.chesiltheatre.org.uk
Salisbury Playhouse
Malthouse Lane, Salisbury.
Tel: 01722 320333;
www.salisburyplayhouse.com
Theatre Royal
21–23 Jewry Street, Winchester.
Tel: 01962 840440;
www.theatre-royal-winchester.co.uk

SPORTS & ACTIVITIES
CYCLE HIRE
Hayball Cyclesport
The Black Horse Chequer, 26–30
Winchester Street, Salisbury.
Tel: 01722 411378;
www.hayball.co.uk

FISHING
Avington Trout Fishery
Avington Estate, Avington.
Tel: 01962 779312;
www.avingtontrout.com
Broadlands Estate
Broadlands, Romsey.
Tel: 01794 518885
HORSE-RIDING
Grovely Riding Centre
Water Ditchampton, Wilton, Salisbury.
Tel: 01722 742288
WALKING
The Itchen Way
A 25-mile (40.2km) walk along
the River Itchen from Cheriton to
Southampton.
The Test Way
A 44-mile (71km) hike from Inkpen
Beacon to Eling Wharf.
The Clarendon Way
A 26-mile (42km) trail from Winchester
to Salisbury.
The Avon Valley Path
A 34-mile (55km) route from Salisbury
to Christchurch.

ANNUAL EVENTS & CUSTOMS
Alresford
Watercress Festival, mid-May.
Romsey
Hampshire County Show,
Broadlands Park, end May.
Tel: 01283 820548;
www.livingheritagecountryshows.co.uk
Romsey Show,
Broadlands Park, early Sep.
Tel: 01794 517521;
www.romseyshow.co.uk
Salisbury
St George's Day, 23 Apr.
Street theatre, pageantry and dragons,
International Arts Festival, mid-May to
mid-Jun. A variety of art related events
to suit all ages
Shaftesbury
Gold Hill Fair, early Jul.
Stalls, music and dancing.
Winchester
Hat Fair, late Jun–early Jul.
Celebration of street theatre.

Grosvenor Hotel
High Street, Stockbridge, SO20 6EU
Tel: 01264 810606

Enjoy a delicious cream tea, or toasted tea cakes with a choice of different teas and coffees, in the comfort of this grand old fishing hotel, which juts into the High Street.

Lillie Langtry's
High Street, Stockbridge, SO20 6HF
Tel: 01264 810954

This old building on the main street was once an inn frequented by actress Lillie Langtry. Today it is a homely tea room, serving crumpets dripping with butter and home-made jam, and scones with clotted cream from a neighbouring Jersey herd. You can also enjoy a light lunch here on the shady terrace by the stream.

Miss Moody's Tea Rooms
King John's House, Church Street, Romsey, SO51 8BT
Tel: 01794 512200

With its home-made coffee cake, fresh flowers on the tables, friendly service and mismatched floral china teacups, this is surely what a country tea room should be like! Miss Mabel Moody ran a tea room here in the 1930s, and the tradition continues, with cream teas in summer and light snacks for lunch. There's a pretty courtyard to sit in, too.

Tiffin Tea Rooms
50 West Street, Alresford, SO24 9AU
Tel: 01962 734394

This friendly, traditional tea room with its blue-and-white striped awning serves home-made cakes, cream teas and speciality teas and coffees.

The Haunch of Venison
1–5 Minster Street, Salisbury, SP1 1TB
Tel: 01722 411313
Craftsmen working on the cathedral
spire were some of the early customers
of this pub, dating back to 1320.
A restaurant in summer serves treats
such as pork with coriander and ginger
and coconut Thai nage. Beers include
Courage Best.

The Mayfly
Testcombe, Stockbridge, SO20 6AZ
Tel: 01264 860283
A lovely old country pub,
the Mayfly looks onto the fast-flowing
River Test. A selection of hot and cold
meats, quiches and pies is laid out
buffet-style, along with a few hot daily
specials. Beers include Ringwood Best
and Wadworth 6X.

The Plough Inn
Main Road, Sparsholt, SO21 2NW
Tel: 01962 776353
Originally the coach house for
Sparsholt Manor, the Plough has been
extended over the years and offers a
harmonious interior decorated with
old farming tools, stone jars and dried
hops to complement the real ales and
good food on offer. One end of the bar
offers light meals, such as tomato and
olive pasta, and chilli and chickpea
cakes, while the far end offers more
serious fare, such as lamb shank.

The Wykeham Arms
75 Kingsgate Street,
Winchester, SO23 9PE
Tel: 01962 853834
The 'Wyk', in an old back street
near Winchester College, is a local
institution. It is furnished in part with
old desks and ephemera from the
school. The food is excellent, ranging
from the Wyk cottage pie, to grilled
sea bass with new potatoes. There is a
choice of around 20 wines by the glass,
and 60 more by the bottle.

TOURIST INFORMATION CENTRES
Bournemouth
Westover Road.
Tel: 0845 051 1700;
www.bournemouth.co.uk
Poole
Enefco House, Poole Quay.
Tel: 01202 253253;
www.pooletourism.com
Swanage
The White House, Shore Road.
Tel: 01929 422885;
www.swanage.gov.uk
Wareham
Holy Trinity Church,
South Street.
Tel: 01929 522740;
www.purbeck.gov.uk
Wimborne
29 High Street.
Tel: 01202 886116;
www.ruraldorset.com

OTHER INFORMATION
New Forest Ranger Service
Forestry Commission, The Queen's
House, Lyndhurst.
Tel: 023 8028 6840;
www.forestry.gov.uk/
newforest

CONSERVATION & HERITAGE ORGANISATIONS
The National Trust (NT)
PO Box 39, Warrington WA5 7WD.
Tel: 0870 458 4000;
www.nationaltrust.org.uk
English Heritage (EH)
PO Box 569
Swindon SN2 2YP.
Tel: 0870 333 1181;
www.english-heritage.org.uk
English Nature (EN)
(Hampshire and Isle of Wight Team)
1 Southampton Road, Lyndhurst,
Hampshire, SO43 7BU.
Tel: 023 8028 6410;
www.english-nature.org.uk

Royal Society for the Protection of Birds (RSPB)
The Lodge, Sandy, Bedfordshire
SG19 2DL
Tel: 01767 680551; www.rspb.org.uk
National Trust (NT)
PO Box 39, Warrington WA5 7WD.
Tel: 0870 458 4000;
www.nationaltrust.org.uk

BEACHES
Lifeguards are generally found on busy beaches during the summer season. Dogs may not be allowed on some beaches during busy summer months.
Coastguard
For Coastguard Assistance dial 999 and ask for the Coastguard Service, which co-ordinates recue services.

PARKING
Information on parking permits and car parks in the area is available from local Tourist Information Centres and on the Web.

PLACES OF INTEREST
For further information about specific places or attractions contact the relevant local TIC or check the Web.

PUBLIC TRANSPORT
Traveline
Tel: 0870 608 2608;
www.traveline.org.uk
Red Funnel Ferries
Town Quay, Southampton
Tel: 0870 444 8898;
www.redfunnel.co.uk
Wight Link Ferries
Tel: 0870 582 774
Hythe Ferry
Tel: 02380 840722;
www.hytheferry.co.uk
Gosport Ferry
Tel: 023 9252 4551;
www.gosportferry.co.uk
Hovertravel
Clarence Esplanade, Southsea.
Tel: 02392 811000;
www.hovertravel.co.uk

WEATHER
www.onlineweather.com

INDEX

INDEX

ACKNOWLEDGEMENTS

The Automobile Association would like to thank the following photographers, companies and picture libraries for their assistance in the preparation of this book.

Abbreviations for the picture credits are as follows – (t) top; (b) bottom; (c) centre; (l) left; (r) right; (AA) AA World Travel Library.

2/3 AA/A Burton; 5 AA/W Voysey; 6/7 AA/W Voysey; 9 AA/J Tims; 11 AA/W Voysey; 13 AA/W Voysey; 14 AA/M Jourdan; 15l AA/S McBride; 15r AA/A Burton; 16l AA/A Burton; 16r AA/A Burton; 17l AA/A Burton; 17r AA/A Burton; 19 AA/A J Hopkins; 20 AA/M Jourdan; 23 AA/S & O Mathews; 24 AA/M Moody; 26 AA/A Burton; 28/29 AA/A Burton; 30 AA/A Burton; 31t AA/A Burton; 31b AA/P Baker; 32 AA/P Enticknap; 33l AA/J Tims; 33r AA/A Burton; 35 AA/A Burton; 39 AA/A Burton; 43 AA/A Burton; 46 AA/R Ireland; 51 AA/A Burton; 54/55 AA/A Burton; 59 AA/W Voysey; 61 AA/P Baker; 67 AA/A Burton; 68 AA/A Burton; 70 AA/A Burton; 72/73 AA/A Burton; 74 AA/A Burton; 75l AA/A Burton; 75r AA/A Burton; 76 AA/A Burton; 77 AA/A Burton; 78 AA/A Burton; 81 AA/A Burton; 82 AA/A Burton; 85 AA/A Burton; 86/87 AA/A Burton; 89 AA/A Burton; 90 AA/A Burton; 93 AA/A Burton; 94/95 AA/W Voysey; 99 AA/A Burton; 100 AA/A Burton; 103 AA/A Burton; 104 AA/A Burton; 106/107 AA/A Burton; 109 AA/A Burton; 110 AA/D Forss; 112/113 AA/R Fletcher; 119 AA/A Burton; 120 AA/A Burton; 122 AA/A Burton; 124/125 AA/A Burton; 126 AA/S McBride; 127 AA/A Burton; 128 AA/A Burton; 129t AA/A Burton; 129b AA/A Burton; 130 AA/A Burton; 133 AA/A Burton; 134 AA/A Burton; 136 AA/A Burton; 138/139 AA/A Burton; 141 AA/S & O Mathews; 143 AA/A Burton; 144 AA/D Forss; 147 AA/D Forss; 149 AA/S McBride; 150/151 AA/A Burton; 153 AA/T Souter; 155 AA/S & O Mathews; 156 AA/A Burton; 158/159 AA/S McBride; 161 AA/A Burton; 162 AA/A Burton; 164/165 AA/S McBride; 171 AA/A Burton; 172 AA/A Burton; 174 AA/A Burton; 176/177 AA/W Voysey; 178 AA; 179l AA/A Burton; 179r AA/A Burton; 181 AA/A Burton; 182 AA/A Burton; 185 AA/W Voysey; 186 AA/A Burton; 189 AA/D Forss; 190/191 AA/W Voysey; 192 AA/A Burton; 194 AA/S Day; 196 AA/A Burton; 198/199 AA/W Voysey; 201 AA/A Burton; 207 AA/A Burton; 208 AA/T Souter; 210 AA/J Tims; 212/213 AA/M Moody; 214 AA/M Moody; 215t AA/M Moody; 215b AA/M Moody; 216 AA/J Tims; 217 AA/J Tims; 219 AA/M Moody; 222 AA/M Moody; 225 AA; 226 AA/A Burton; 230 AA/J Tims; 234/235 AA/J Tims; 238/239 AA/M Moody; 241 AA/M Moody; 247 AA/J Tims; 248 AA/M Moody

Every effort has been made to trace the copyright holders, and we apologise in advance for any accidental errors. We would be happy to apply the corrections in the following edition of this publication.